THE JOURNAL JURISPRUDENCE

VOLUME TWENTY-THREE

CONTRIBUTORS

Professor Richard A. Westin
University of Kentucky College of Law

Dr Don Stacy, M.D. dABR
Independent Scholar

Mr Joshua Nguyen
Loyola University New Orleans

Professor Walter E. Block
Loyola University New Orleans

Mr C.G. Bateman
University of British Columbia

EDITOR

Dr Aron Ping D'Souza
Stawell Chambers, Melbourne

MICHAELMAS TERM
SEPTEMBER 2014

Elias Clark

PUBLISHED BY THE ELIAS CLARK GROUP
DISTRIBUTED IN CONNECTION WITH THE GALE GROUP,
A PART OF CENGAGE LEARNING

The Elias Clark Group
www.elias-clark.com

GPO Box 5001
Melbourne, Victoria 3001
Australia

First Published 2014.

Cataloguing-in-Publication entry

Editor: D'Souza, Aron Ping.
Westin, Richard A.
Stacy, Don.
Nguyen, Joshua.
Block, Walter E.
Bateman, C.G.

Title: The Journal Jurisprudence, Volume Twenty-Three.

ISBN: 978-0-9924143-1-3 (pbk.)
ISSN: 1836-0955

Subjects: Law – jurisprudence.
Philosophy – general.

This edition may be cited as

(2014) J. Juris.

followed by the page number

ABOUT THE TYPEFACE

The Journal Jurisprudence is typeset in Garamond 12 and the footnotes are set in Garamond 10. The typeface was named for Claude Garamond (c. 1480 - 1561) and are based on the work of Jean Jannon. By 1540, Garamond became a popular choice in the books of the French imperial court, particularly under King Francis I. Garamond was said to be based on the handwriting of Angelo Vergecio, a librarian to the King. The italics of Garamond are credited to Robert Grandjon, an assistant to Claude Garamond. The font was re-popularised in the art deco era and became a mainstay on twentieth-century publication. In the 1970s, the font was redesigned by the International Typeface Corporation, which forms the basis of the variant of Garamond used in this Journal.

TABLE OF CONTENTS

CALL FOR PAPERS

The field of jurisprudence lies at the nexus of law and politics, the practical and the philosophical. By understanding the theoretical foundations of law, jurisprudence can inform us of the place of legal structures within larger philosophical frameworks. In its inaugural edition, *The Journal Jurisprudence* received many creative and telling answers to the question, "What is Law?" For the second edition, the editors challenged the scholarly and lay communities to inquire into intersection between jurisprudence and economics.

With the backing of our diverse and disparate community, *The Journal Jurisprudence* has now evolved into a distinct format. We will no longer be setting a question for each issue, but instead designing issues around the articles we received. Therefore, we invite scholars, lawyers, judges, philosophers and lay people to tackle any and all of the great questions of law. Knowing that ideas come in all forms, papers can be of any length, although emphasis is placed on readability by lay audiences.

Papers may engage with case studies, intellectual arguments or any other method that answers philosophical questions applicable to the law. Importantly, articles will be selected based upon quality and the readability of works by non-specialists. The intent of the Journal is to involve non-scholars in the important debates of legal philosophy.

The Journal also welcomes and encourages submissions of articles typically not found in law journals, including opinionated or personalised insights into the philosophy of law and its applications to practical situations.

Jurisprudence is published four times per year, to coincide with the four terms of the legal year, in an attractive paperback and electronic edition.

Each author who submits to this volume will be provided with a complimentary copy of the journal.

Length: Any length is acceptable, although readability to non-specialist is key.

Presentation Style: Papers must comply with the Australian Guide to Legal Citations, Second Edition published by the Melbourne University Law Review. An electronic edition is available at, http://mulr.law.unimelb.edu.au/PDFs/aglc_dl.pdf

Submission: You must submit electronically in Microsoft Word format to editor@jurisprudence.com.au. Extraneous formatting is discouraged.

Correspondence can also be sent to this address. If you are considering submitting an article, you are invited to contact the editor to discuss ideas before authoring a work.

SUBSCRIPTION INFORMATION

The Journal is published four times per year in an attractive softcover book. Subscription to the Journal can be achieved by two methods:

1) Single issues can be purchased on amazon.com. Our publishers, the Elias Clark Group, set a retail price for each edition, typically AU$40. However, due to their agreement with amazon.com, the price may vary for retail customers.

2) A subscription to the Journal can be purchased for AU$150 per year, or AU$280 for two years. This price includes postage throughout the world. Payment can be made by international bank cheque, but not a personal cheque, to:

The Journal Jurisprudence,
C/o The Elias Clark Group
GPO Box 5001
Melbourne, Victoria, Australia.

Alternatively, the Journal is available online at www.jurisprudence.com.au and can be read there free of charge.

THE HISTORICAL ORIGINS OF PROGRESSIVE TAXATION

Richard A. Westin[1]

Thus, in practice, we usually find some economists testify before legislators in the morning that wealth should be distributed to make the dicta of welfare economics ethically acceptable. At the same time, other economists in the afternoon will testify before the same legislators that such wealth distributions beget inefficiencies - the little deadweight loss triangles we had studied – and these should be avoided.

Uwe Reinhardt [2]

BACKGROUND

American federal income tax rates run in cycles, generally rising during wars, and then declining. Over the span of America's history, the top wartime rates peaked at 94% during World War Two,[3] then 90%, after which they declined in steps to a nadir of 28% in the early years of Ronald Reagan. Since then they have risen slightly to the present modest 39.6% rate, buttressed by some intricate phase-outs,[4] a fairly toothless alternative minimum tax[5] designed to assure that even the sharpest tax-avoider will contribute at least something to the federal government's coffers and a small tax on investment income of wealthy taxpayers[6]. There is also a significant federal estate tax that affects a

[1] Professor of law, University of Kentucky College of Law. My thanks to William T. Loomis, Franklin Runge, Stephen Salant, Stephen Vasek, Roger Tolbert, and tip of the hat to Joseph Bankman.

[2] From what appears to be a class handout at Princeton University, prepared for a course in microeconmics, captioned How Microeconomists Bastardized Benthamite Utilitarianism, available at http://www.princeton.edu/~reinhard/pdfs/100-NEXT_HOW_ECONOMISTS_BASTARDIZED_BENTHAMITE_UTILITARIANISM.pdf

[3] Individual Income Tax Act of 1944, Pub. L. No. 315, 58 Stat. 231. However, §12(g) provided that the effective rate could not exceed 90 percent. Id. § 12(g). As with all comparisons of differing tax rates over time, the tax base seems always to vary as the tax law evolves, making comparisons invariably imperfect. Hereinafter, references to sections are to the Internal Revenue Code of 1986, as amended, unless otherwise indicated ("IRC").

[4] E.g., IRC's § 67 (2% floor on certain itemized deductions) and IRC § 151(d)(3)(A) (phase-out of personal exemptions).

[5] IRC § 55. It is somewhat toothless because the tax is largely creditable against regular income taxes in years when the taxpayer owes only regular taxes.

[6] The investment income tax rate is 3.8 % and applies only to individuals with large incomes.

small percentage of taxpayers and is easily gamed.[7] However, these transfer taxes do add progressivity to the tax system.[8]

The normal cycle has recently changed in that Congress has declined to pay for America's recent undeclared wars with tax increases, while favoring high income taxpayers in the form of relatively low top rate of taxation on ordinary income and a modest 20 percent top rate of taxation on long-term capital gains and many dividends.[9] At the scandalous edge of this new picture, wily hedge fund managers have learned how to convert income from services into long-term capital gains via the "carried interest."[10]

The recent popular calls for increasing top rates rely on notions of fairness, which calls are commonly denounced as "class warfare" and foolish diversions of the flow of capital that would otherwise support business activity. The claim of "fairness" is often pooh-poohed as merely intuitive and is countered with proposals for flat taxes, value-added taxes and technical criticisms of progressive taxation.[11] The debate is unsophisticated to put it mildly. Laymen and the press seem unable to get past simplistic debates, and as a result, conversations about appropriate rates seem bankrupt.

It seems we suffer from amnesia about Western history. The concept of imposing taxes at increasing rates as income or wealth rises has a history that spans over two thousand years, and a large literature. The most interesting feature is that if one looks at the point of origin, at least in the West, theorizing about taxes begins in Classical Greece, with a focus on societal virtue in a collective moral sense, then moves to Eighteenth Century mathematicians who turned to what are now called microeconomic (or Utilitarian) theories of maximizing societal welfare, and ends today with materialistic, insipid debates that fall far short of the profundity of thinking that evolved in the distant past. In fact, the theories bandied about today are largely rhetorical.

The principles underlying progressive taxation have been with us at least since Aristotle's time. Progressive taxation has an impressive pedigree and yet its history never creeps into the debate. Perhaps that failure is in part because American casebooks on Federal

---

7 IRC § 2001; it is buttressed by a complementary gift tax for inter vivos transfers (IRC §2501) and a generation-skipping transfer tax (IRC § 2601). The top rate is 40% for 2013-2014. The seminal article on the weakness of the transfer taxes is George Cooper, A Voluntary Tax? New Perspectives on Sophisticated Estate Tax Avoidance, 77 Colum. L. Rev. 161 (1977).

8 See Graetz, To Praise the Estate Tax, Not to Bury It, 93 Yale LJ 259 (1983).

9 IRC §1(h). The computations are extremely complicated and capital gains rates in fact range from 0% to 20%, as income rises.

10 See, e.g., David Weisbach, The Taxation of Carried Interests in Private Equity, 94 Va. L. Rev. 715 (2008).

11 The best known of the criticisms is a short book by Walter Blum and Harry Kalven, The Uneasy Case for Progressive Taxation (The University of Chicago Press, 1963).

income taxation always seem to begin in 1913 with the passage of the Sixteenth Amendment.

The purpose of this article is to trace the history of progressive taxation from Greece to today's contentious battles in Washington, with a main stop at the Enlightenment. A clear inference of this writing is that the furious debates in Congress and the press over progressive taxation go on in a vacuum, bereft of historical context or any recognition of the great contributions of sincere thinkers in the past and how those deep thinkers preferred progressive taxation in some form or other.

Some caveats are in order. First, progressive taxation nowadays usually refers to increasing marginal tax rates as taxpayers' taxable incomes rise, but there are also progressive taxes on wealth or transfers of wealth. When I refer to progressive taxes the meaning will vary with the times. For example, ancient Greece had surrogates for wealth taxes in the form of liturgies. Eighteenth Century Britain had a hodge-podge of taxes, but only briefly was there an income tax and there was no inheritance tax. Perhaps the simplest way to define the term is "rising levels of taxation as the ability to pay rises." Another caveat is that thinking about progressive taxation is often blended with notions of how to distribute tax revenues. As will be seen, a number of leading thinkers consider the combination the important topic, not just the revenues.

Classical Athens

Today's dialogues about progressive taxation sometimes suggest the very idea is novel and possibly even shocking. In fact, the progressive taxation has a visible genesis in ancient Greece, where it was actually practiced, but in forms that are so different from today's practices that one has to dig deep to find it. Most importantly from the point of view tracing the history of progressive taxation as a principle, Aristotle's deep thoughts on the matter presage the thinking of Adam Smith and Jeremy Bentham during the Enlightenment where formal notions of progressive taxation first took hold and considered both revenues and their distribution.

It appears that in general, Athenian citizens historically considered paying taxes something a citizen did as a matter of civic pride. According to one scholar, who found the lack of coherent information on Greek taxes dismaying, there was one constant over time:

> "Until the establishment of democracies, political activity made few financial demands, and they were usually met by the very aristocracy of birth and wealth which monopolized all governmental functions. Timocratic systems, like the one introduced by Solon in Athens . . . defined which property classes (tele) had

> access to magistracies. They nonetheless maintained the principle that possession of wealth and public duty were inseparable. Thus, the age-old Greek creed, that performance of public functions bears a resemblance to the liturgies of the post-Classical period, when these were increasingly absorbed by regular magistracies."[12]

During Greece's Classical period (480 BC and 323 BC), or Athenian Empire, Athens was justly famous for new ideas and a fresh spirit of inquiry, with thought emanating from first principles, honestly sought and developed. The focus was largely on moral and ethical issues, but there was also an opposing forensic side provided by the Sophists. In college classrooms Classical Greece is the usual starting point for the study of Western civilization, so this article starts there. Although many of the accepted norms are offensive to modern values – such as acceptance of slavery and the subordination of women – there is no doubt that education flourished in the form of colonies of private academies and that literacy rapidly increased.[13] Perhaps a good measure of the power of education was that Socrates' open-minded thinking became so provocative that the authorities felt it necessary to execute him allegedly on the grounds of impiety and corrupting youth, but really for his provocative philosophical inquiries.

Not everyone complied. One can detect this in the following famous passage from *The Republic* in which Socrates (469 BC to 399 BC) debates the Sophist, Thrasymachus, who exposes what most people consider a horrible truth:

> "The just man is always a loser, my naïve Socrates. He always loses out to the unjust. Consider private business. If a just man takes an unjust man for a partner and the partnership is later dissolved, it is invariably the unjust man who walks away with the lion's share of the assets. Consider their dealings with government. When taxes fall due, the just man will pay more and the unjust less on the same amount of property. Or, if the government is letting out contracts or disbursing money for some other purpose, those who are unjust will get it all and the just will get nothing. The just man in public office will reap no rewards. In the first place, as he conscientiously attends to the affairs of the state, he must necessarily have little time left to attend to his own affairs. His principles forbid him to embezzle on his own account. They will also prevent him from handing out unlawful favors from the public treasury to others. In consequence, he will earn

---

[12] A Companion to Ancient Greek Government (Beck Ed., Blackwell 2013) p. 333 (chapter by Vincent Gabrielson).

[13] *Classical Athens,* The Oxford Encyclopedia of Ancient Greece and Rome (Oxford Univ. Press 2012, Michael Gagarin, editor), available at http://www.oxfordreference.com.ezproxy.uky.edu/view/10.1093/acref/9780195170726.001.0001/acref-9780195170726-e-408?rskey=cYPPW9&result=407.

> the enmity of his disappointed friends and acquaintances."[14]

There was no formal study of economics as we know it, but Aristotle (384 BC – 322 BC) made major inroads into the subject[15] especially in *The Topics*, and Chapter 1 of Book 7 of his *Politics,* which contain an early rationale for progressive taxation and a starting point for the study of Utilitarianism. Here are the famous words:

> "[E]xternal goods have a limit, like any other instrument, and all things useful are of such a nature that where there is too much of them they must either do harm, or at any rate be of no use"[16]

He disliked greed, associating it with a lack of virtue.

> "Since the unjust person is greedy, he will be concerned with goods -- not all goods, but with those with which good and bad fortune are concerned; these are always good without qualification, but not always for a particular individual. (People pray for and pursue these things, but they should not; rather, they should pray that those goods that are good without qualification may also be good for them, and they should choose things that are good for them.)"[17]

In modern economic parlance, the marginal utility (incremental value) of anything, including money, declines as its quantity increases in the hands of a human being. The implication is that at the outer reaches of wealth or income, not receiving more of it does not hurt, and might well be a blessing. As applied to income taxation, it implies that as income rises the personal suffering from any given level of tax declines, and implicitly argues in favor of a progressive tax rate rather than a proportionate (flat) rate.

Aristotle drew on his teacher, Plato (roughly 428 BC to 347 BC). Plato's *Laws*[18] include a foray into distributive taxation that many readers may find alarming. Essentially, he asserted through a literary persona, the Athenian stranger, that in an ideal circumstance no citizen should have more than four times the wealth of the least of the citizenry.[19]

---

14 Plato, Republic Book I, Richard Sterling, (William Scott eds. 1958), p 343 *d,e* (1985) (original pagination).

15 See generally, Scott Meikle, Aristotle's' Economic Thought (Clarendon Paperbacks 1995).

16 Aristotle, Politics, Book VII Chapter 1. Aristotle's scrupulous scientific thought and careful reasoning still influence the social sciences and humanities; he apparently invented the syllogism.

17 Book 5, Nicomachean Ethics, Roger Crisp, (Cambridge University Press, 2000), p. 1129 (original pagination).

18 Plato's teacher was Socrates; his student was Aristotle. Aristotle's most famous pupil was Alexander the Greek who burst out of Macedonia as a teenager and went on to conquer the bulk of the then known world.

19 Plato, Laws, in Dialogues, 348 BC, Translated by Benjamin Jowett (4th ed., Oxford, Clarendon Press,

The concept is that in the new Utopian Cretan city of Magnesia, each citizen would receive an initial allotment of nontransferable, non-mortgageable land, good in perpetuity. Four times the value of the lot would be the limit of anyone else's wealth.[20] The overly prosperous could give away their surplus to the local government or to the gods, but if not, then the excess would be expropriated. The underlying reason for this would be to prevent "distraction" that arises from civil conflict and disconcerting differences in wealth between rich and poor. For Plato good life is one of virtue through which human beings attain happiness, which seems a pleasant mixture of hedonism and morality. The format of the essay is a discussion among three astute men, Cleinias, from the Cretan city of Cnossos, Megillus, from Sparta, and a nameless stranger from Athens who will collectively found Magnesia, a city designed to nurture the human soul.

It is the stranger – concerned with revenues and redistribution -- who recommends that there be a limit on the amount of wealth a household may accumulate. Special magistrates would assess the value of the land, buildings, and equipment needed to cultivate the land — the basic allotment. Curiously, outsiders such as artisans and merchants excluded from citizenship would be exempt, apparently as a necessary nuisance. On the other hand, aliens could generally reside in Magnesia for no more than 20 years and unlike the citizens would not qualify for Magnesia's generous social safety net. Here are the words of the Athenian stranger — Plato in disguise one imagines:

> "The form of law which I should propose as the natural sequel would be as follows: In a state which is desirous of being saved from the greatest of all plagues — not faction, but rather distraction; — there should exist among the citizens neither extreme poverty, nor, again, excess of wealth, for both are productive of both these evils. Now the legislator should determine what is to be the limit of poverty or wealth.
>
> Let the limit of poverty be the value of the lot; this ought to be preserved, and no ruler, nor anyone else who aspires after a reputation for virtue, will allow the lot to be impaired in any case. This the legislator gives as a measure, and he will permit a man to acquire double or triple, or as much as four times the amount of this.
>
> But if a person have yet greater riches, whether he has found them, or they have been given to him, or he has made them in business, or has acquired by any stroke of fortune that which is in excess of the measure, if he give back the surplus to the state, and to the Gods who are the patrons of the state, he shall

1953), Book IV

[20] There seems to be some ambiguity as to how the 400% amount is valued and exactly what its base is.

> suffer no penalty or loss of reputation; but if he disobeys this our law anyone who likes may inform against him and receive half the value of the excess, and the delinquent shall pay a sum equal to the excess out of his own property, and the other half of the excess shall belong to the Gods. And let every possession of every man, with the exception of the lot, be publicly registered before the magistrates whom the law appoints, so that all suits about money may be easy and quite simple."[21]

The Sophists were a diametrically opposite force. They operated during the 5th century BC, for about the same period as that spanned by the lives of Socrates and Aristotle. By trade the Sophists were itinerant debaters, proto-lawyers and teachers who frequented Greek cities, offering young wealthy Greek males an education, always for a fee, especially in rhetorical persuasion. Plato and Aristotle, among others, found them offensive because they placed so much emphasis on argumentation and so little on morality and religion, and reviled them for demanding payment for education.[22] Nowadays, the term *sophistry* has come to mean the unscrupulous use of fallacious reasoning and intellectual charlatanism. Like the modern "spin doctors" of Washington, DC, they were especially skilled at selecting words that would most move their audience.

> "Sophists did, however, have one important thing in common: whatever else they did or did not claim to know, they characteristically had a great understanding of what words would entertain or impress or persuade an audience." [23]

Many scholars consider them a natural outgrowth of the modernization of Greece of the day into a more democratic and litigious society which required people who could argue well, and credit them with having open minds. The most famous of the Sophists, Protagoros, exemplifies this honest side; he was found guilty of impiety for saying he knew nothing of the gods because of his limitations as a human and the complexity of the question. He soon thereafter died in a shipwreck.[24]

Taxes in Ancient Greece

21 Plato's student, Aristotle, staked out a similar position in Politics, where he discussed the issue of excess property, considering that the right to property is limited to what is enough to maintain the households and life that the polis produces. See fn 19, above at pg 313-14.

22 See *The Sophist,* a dialogue likely penned in 360 B.C.

23 Introduction To Protagoras, (Plato), (Nicholas Denyer ed.) (Cambridge University Press, 2008) p.1. A recent example of effective rhetorical use of language includes "junk science" to attack the scientific underpinnings of global warming and "job killer" to describe a change in the tax law that could adversely affect employment and "death panels" to describe risk of socialized medicine.

24 The Cambridge Dictionary of Philosophy, (Audi, Ed. 1995) p.752.

To summarize what is about to come, the tax system was progressive in that the burden of government fell heavily on the wealthy, but there were a variety of other levies that primarily fell on commercial activities. The taxes varied city-by-city. The following discussion only covers Athens. The extent to which the philosophers' thoughts on progressive taxation might have influenced lawmakers seems unknown.

The earliest records of the tax system appear in Solon's reforms, around 594 BC, during the time of the tyrants, meaning one-man rule, but not necessarily a harsh rule.[25] Solon's reforms separated the Athenian people into four categories based on agricultural production. This was one of the early graded flat tax systems, as each class paid a tax that correlated with the amount of agricultural production.[26]

> "Solon made four classes, a number afterwards adopted by Plato in his Work on Laws . . . The first class was the Pentacosiomedimini; that is to say, those who received 500 measures, either dry or liquid, from their lands, medimini of dry, and metretae of liquid measure. For the second class he took those who received 300 measures, and could afford to keep a horse, viz. a war-horse, to which was assessed another for a servant, and they must also necessarily have required a yoke of animals; this class was called Knights. The third class are the Zeugitae, and their valuation is called the valuation of the Zeugiate . . . Their income is stated in general at 200 measures of dry and liquid measure. The last class is the Thetes, whose valuation was less than Zeugitae. 'The Pentacosiomedimini', says Pollux, 'expended upon the public weal one talent, the second 30 minas, the third 10 minas, and the Thetes nothing.'"[27]

During the time of the tyrants wealth was determined on the basis of visible agricultural production, which often represented the taxpayer's wealth unfairly.[28] Kleisthene's reforms of the tax system began in 508-507 BC.[29] Under his system, the citizenry chose a council of 500 citizens called the Boule whose job it was to identify rich citizens who would be singled out for taxation.

---

25 It fell within the Archaic ("old fashioned") period in Greece, which spanned the period 800 BC to 480 BC).

26 Lyttkens, Carl Hampus, Rational-Actor Prospective on the Origin of Liturgies in Ancient Greece, *Journal of Institutional and Theoretical Economics*, Vol. 153, No. 3 (Sept. 1997) pp. 462

27 Boeckh, August, The Public Economy of Athens, in four books; to which is added, A dissertation on the silver-mines of Laurion, Volume II, John Murray pp.259-61 (London, 1828). The primary source of historical information about Solon is likely Plutarch's Lives. A famous version is The Lives of the Noble Grecians, by Plutarch, translated by John Dryden et. al. (1683).

28 Kaiser, Brooks A., The Athenian Trierarchy: Mechanism Design for the Private Provision of Public Goods, The Journal of Economic History, Vol. 67 No. 2 (Jun., 2007), p. 448

29 Id. At 448-49

One might think of it as an early whistle-blower system in which the reward was the absence of taxation. It also has the flavor of a "shotgun buy sell agreement."[30] Aside from of a variety of miscellaneous taxes on such things as commerce and professions, a major sources of Athens' revenue came from "liturgies," whose purpose was to induce wealthy private citizens pay for public services, [31] in which the contributors generally took civic pride. The obligations came in two basic forms; festival liturgies and trierarchies. The assignment of liturgies was administered by magistrates, who initially solicited volunteers for the liturgies. After the supply of volunteers ran out, the remaining liturgies were assigned to whomever the magistrates considered wealthy enough to bear their costs. An interesting aspect of the law was that the citizens who were assigned liturgies were empowered to use the antidosis system to shift the burden onto a citizen that was found wealthier.[32]

The process of antidosis was as follows:

> "[V]isible wealth determined whether or not an individual actually carried out the service or attempted the antidosis challenge to avoid it instead. This challenge allowed an individual charged with performing a [tax] the opportunity to prove another individual more fit (wealthier) to carry it out. The mechanism was clever; if an individual challenged another in the antidosis, the challenged citizen had three choices. He might agree he was indeed wealthier . . . and perform the [tax] himself. If the challenged citizen did not agree, two choices remained. He might simply have offered to swap his visible wealth for that of his challenger's, and the challenger would have to perform the [tax] with this new level of wealth. Alternatively, he might rather have the court decide, based on an investigation of wealth. In that case, the court would designate either the challenger or the challenged citizen (each one facing the probability of being selected); the selected one would have to keep his own wealth and perform the [tax]."[33]

Festival liturgies were used to stage festivals for the citizens of Athens, the best known of which were the Choreiga (dramatic productions).[34] Initially the wealthy volunteered as

---

30 Such agreements are common in small businesses. They permit one owner to come forward with a formal offer. The offeree can then decide if he wants to accept or instead exercise his right to buy the co-owner's share at the same price.

31 Christ, Matthew, Liturgy Avoidance and Antidosis in Classical Athens. Transactions of the American Philological Association (1974-), Vol. 120 (1990), pp. 148 published by Johns Hopkins university press.

32 Christ, Liturgy Avoidance and Antidosis, at 149-50. It is not clear which statesman first enacted this system. According to Financing the Athenian Fleet: Public Taxation and Social Relations p. 94 (Vincent Gabrielsen,, Johns Hopkins University Press, 2010), it was attributed to Solon when it was liked and to Isocrates when disliked.

33 Id. At 449-50

34 Lyttkens at 462.

a great honor was conferred on whoever took on liturgies and often those who put on the liturgies were given high positions in the government.[35] The amount of the liturgy depended on the cost of the event itself, (as high as 3,000 drachmae).[36] After completing a festival liturgy the "donors" were exempt for the next year.[37]

The Trierarchy was an expensive military public contribution, amounting to taxation and highly visible distribution. Each citizen who performed a Trierarchy paid for the commissioning and command of a state warship, as well as its crew for a year. These were more expensive than the festival liturgies, generally costing anywhere from 4,000 to 6,000 drachmae.[38] A person who performed a Trierarchy was exempt from performance for the following two years.[39] Those who defaulted on these obligations were not treated like public debtors; rather the obligation to repay was controlled entirely by private citizens. The next person selected to perform was responsible for recovering the naval equipment from the defaulting debtor. The collection process began with persuasion, but the courts were called in if persuasion failed.[40]

The tax system later became more advanced and broader-based with the development of the Eisphora. This was a direct tax on the wealthy used to finance military campaigns. The first known Eisphora was in 428 to sustain military operations at Mytilene.[41] Prior to 378-9 BC, the amounts and taxpayers were determined by the ecclesia (citizens assembly) with each taxpayer paying the same rate as their peers.[42] Thereafter, the tax was administered by military generals. There were taxes upon two different groups, the Metics (non-citizens) and the citizens. The Metics were placed into groups with registrars assigned to them to administer the tax. Each member of the group provided the registrar with an assessment of his wealth. This assessment was scrutinized and sometimes challenged. Once the assessment of wealth was approved, each person had to pay an amount based on his wealth,[43] with different citizens taxed differently:

> "wealthy citizens liable to the [E]isphora were divided into 100 tax-paying groups known as symmories, each with some fifteen members (*symmoritai*). Each of these

35 Id. at 463.

36 Christ, Liturgy Avoidance at 148.

37 Christ, Matthew R., The Evolution of Eisphora in Classical Athens, *The Classical Quarterly*, Vol. 57, No. 1 (May 2007) pg. 57

38 Kaiser at 449.

39 Christ, Evolution of Eisphora at 57

40 Hunter, Virginia, Policing Public Debtors in Classical Athens, *Phoenix*, Vol. 54, No. ½ (Spring-Summer, 2000) p. 31.

41 Christ, Evolution of Esiphora at 53-54

42 Id. at 59.

43 Thomsen, Rudi, Eisphora: A study of direct taxation in Ancient Athens pp. 11 (Gylendalske Boghandel, 1964); Christ, Evolution of Eisphora at 62.

groups was probably responsible for one-hundredth of the total sum levied on citizens by the Assembly on any particular occasion; within each group, individuals paid shares of the group's liability in proportion to their level of wealth, as determined on the basis of their current declarations of their assets."

In order to collect the taxes at a faster rate, Athens, soon thereafter, developed the system of Proeisphora, under which the three wealthiest members of each symmoria were responsible for paying the tax of the entire group consisting of the 300 wealthiest citizens identified by the citizens of Athens from which the citizen could only escape through antidosis.[44] Each of the three wealthiest men then turn towards their 100 members to exact contributions. This process was used both for Trierarchies, which were for extraordinary needs, and for regular property taxes, which taxes were apparently unpopular even though apparently progressive, because they could lead to private financial ruin.[45]

Over time the taxation system became more complex and matured in a way that allowed the determination of wealth to be more accurate. The structure of the system allowed for self-regulation by the people. If a wealthy man hid his wealth, his deception would likely be brought out thorough the antidosis system by another citizen who felt he was being unfairly required to pay or perform a liturgy. The collection efforts were done by those who had already paid the debt to the state and thus were almost entirely a private matter outside of courts.

To sum up their practices, Ancient Greece forced exactions from the rich to support military and civic activities and did so in a systematic and apparently transparent manner. Beyond that simple statement lies a confusing landscape of property taxes as well as a mass of other sources of revenues, including tribute, court fees, confiscations, harbor taxes, and customs and excise duties. [46]

In contrast to ancient Greece, industrialized countries rely primarily on income taxes, in large measure because annual taxes on wealth – whether extracted in cash or service – invite enormous administrative difficulties because of the need to generate honest period appraisals of taxpayers' worth. It seems that Ancient Greece overcame those difficulties by means of several factors: the clever system of antidosis that made lying dangerous; a small population that was aware of each other's economic situations; and, the pride taken

---

[44] Thomsen at 210-12

[45] See (Sept. 1997) pp. 462

[45] Boeckh, August, The Public Economy of Athens, in four books; to which is added, A dissertation on the silver-mines of Laurion, Volume II, John Murray, principally at pp.285-316 (London, 1828). Boeckh considers that historians' understandings of the facts differ widely on this subject.

[46] Id. Pages 3-4 contain a brief summary of the sources of revenue.

in being known for putting on a drama or funding a trireme as well, perhaps, as general civic pride. Income taxes generally have the inequitable feature of taxing people when they have very good years, but not crediting them for bad years.[47] In contrast, wealth taxes apply with an equal hand every year.[48]

Continental Europe Many Years Later

The first tax on income in Continental Europe reportedly appeared in Renaissance Italy[49] and later in Seventeenth and Eighteenth Century France and Holland, but the modern genesis of progressive income taxation is thought to begin in late eighteenth century Britain.[50] Because the topic of Continental taxes never seems to work its way into the American tax dialogue, it is passed over here, except to point out the contributions of a few Continental mathematicians to early Utility Theory.

Bethamite Utilitarianism and the Enlightenment in England

Modestly progressive income taxes have a surprisingly long history in England, perhaps the first of which was Henry II's "Saladin tithe" in 1188 to help fund the unfortunate Third Crusade. It applied at a rate of a tenth of the personal income and moveable property of English laypersons.[51] Crusaders were exempt from the tax. The need arose from the capture of Jerusalem by Saladin at the Battle of Hattin the year before. In 1435 and 1450, in the midst of the Hundred Years War, there was a graduated income tax on propertied individuals, with a minimum rate of 2½%, on incomes under £100 (under £20 in the 1450 tax) rising to 10% on larger incomes.[52] It appears there was another income tax at rate of 10% on people with incomes over £100 to fund wars with Holland and France,[53] as well as a punitive 10% income tax around 1665 on people who bore

[47] Business losses may be carried forwards and backwards to level income under U.S. federal tax law (IRC § 172), but there is no analog for investment loses.

[48] The topic of annual wealth taxes has had a sudden revival, thanks to French economics professor Thomas Piketty. His most recent work is Capital in the Twenty-First Century (Cambridge, MA: Belknap Press, 2014).

[49] Roughly the 14th through 17th Centuries, generally spreading northward from Italy.

[50] See Assaf Likhovski, "A Map of Society: Defining Income in British, British-Colonial and American Tax Legislation" British Tax Review,158-179,(2005), citing inter alia E.R.A. Seligman, The Income Tax (Macmillan, 1911), M. J. Braddick, The Nerves of the State (Manchester University Press, Manchester, 1996); M. Touzery, "Les origines de l'impôt sur le revenu en France: de la monarchie aux républicains radicaux (XVIIIe — XIXe siècles)" (1997).

[51] Peter Harris (2006). *Income tax in common law jurisdictions: from the origins to 1820, Volume 1*. p. 34.

[52] John Lubbbock, THE INCOME TAX IN ENGLAND p. 152. John Lubbock (he North American Review, February 1894).

[53] England, 1642-1791 (Henry Smith Williams editor, 1908). P. 159. Peter Harris. INCOME TAX IN COMMON LAW JURISDICTIONS, VOL. 1 (CAMBRIDGE UNIN. PRESS 2006) p.139.

arms as Royalists.[54] There may have been others as well, but it was not until the Enlightenment that the foundation for progressive taxation was formalized.

The Enlightenment, another of the great eras of open inquiry into seemingly every aspect of science and philosophy, fundamentally revised the underlying principles on which social and political order were founded, and included formalizing the notion of the declining marginal utility of money, but it only tangentially dealt with the theory with respect to taxes, although it did so with force. (The Enlightenment period roughly spanning the 150 years between Hobbes' *Leviathan* in 1651 and the French Revolution in 1798). It was in this period that the modern concepts of the social contract and modern democracy got its start. It is America's political taproot, and remains an intellectual wonder of the world.

The main taxes during the late Enlightenment, when Utility theory was born in England, were those on revenues from the ownership of property, customs duties, stamp taxes and various excises, with excises gradually replacing taxes on the ownership of property. All of these taxes had the potential for being imposed on a progressive basis, but they were not. However, unlike the inflammatory taxes imposed and brutally "farmed" by rapacious agents of the King in France, and to a much lesser degree on the American Colonies, they were imposed so expediently that they avoided general public objection.[55] The excise taxes were particularly attractive because they were assessed on a small number of large producers:

> "There was again, an administrative rationale, for the excise was collected by efficient bureaucrats rather than lay commissioners (as with the assessed and land taxes) or sinecurists (as with the customs). Excise officers were paid salaries rather than fees, promoted on merit with a pension on retirement, and controlled and inspected by a hierarchy of gaugers and surveyors under the general supervision of a central Board of Commissioners."[56]

There was not what we would recognize as a graduated tax on income until 1798 (modified in 1799) when Great Britain enacted an income tax to pay for weapons and equipment in preparation for the Napoleonic Wars.[57] This graduated income tax began at a rate of 2 old pence per pound (.0083 %) on incomes over £60, rising rapidly to a maximum of 2 shillings (10%) per Pound on incomes over £200. The British income tax

---

54 Id at 159.

55 Martin Daunton, TRUSTING LEVIATHAN, Chapter 1(Cambridge University Press 2001) ("TRUSTING LEVIATHAN"). The book is an excellent resource for studying the evolution of British taxes over the period 1799 to 1914, but provides context in discussions of other periods.

56 Trusting Leviathan, p.36.

57 Id. at p. 44. It provided 28% of the additional revenue needed to finance the conflict with revolutionary France and the Napoleonic Wars. Id. at p.45.

was reinstated during the years 1811-1815 to again finance the Napoleonic Wars.[58] It was explicitly a war tax and was repealed when the war ended.[59] It was reinstated in 1842.[60] England's first inheritance tax was not enacted until 1871.[61] In contrast to taxes in the days of the Enlightenment, current American federal taxes fall primarily on income and employment.

Back to Aristotle and his observation about the declining value of goods as their quantities rise ("declining marginal utility of money" in the language of microeconomists). It seems that his observation was not picked up during the Renaissance, but instead emerged under its own steam from the minds of extraordinary mathematicians of a later era who turned their attention to economics. The first hint appears to be from the pen of a Swiss mathematician by the name of Gabriel Cramer[62] in a private letter written in 1728. However, the theory of diminishing marginal utility of money was not formally written up publicly until 1738, when it appeared in "Specimen Theoriae Novae de Mensura Sortis" (Exposition of a New Theory on the Measurement of Risk)[63] by the Swiss scientist and mathematician Daniel Bernoulli, in 1738.[64] Curiously, both Bernoulli and Cramer derived their insight from studying an obscure paradox involving gambling that still interests economists.[65] The study led them to draw

---

58 Id atp.p. 26-42. A chart on p.35 indicates that the income tax became a permanent feature of the tax system in 1851.

59 HM Revenue & Customs, "A tax to beat Napoleon". HM Revenue & Customs. Retrieved 2007-01-24. http://archive.is/gAGX

60 Trusting Leviathan p. 26

61 Id. at p. 35.

62 1704 – 1752. His life is chronicled in W. W. Rouse Ball, A Short Account Of The History of Mathematics, 2d ed. p. 338 (Macmillan, 1893). His wide-ranging interests included a study of why planetary motions are elliptical. In addition to being a mathematician he is credited with being a physicist. His principal academic appointment was in Geneva. His writings clearly show him to believe in the declining marginal utility of money. Cramer's life is chronicled by Walter William Rouse Ball, *A Short Account of the History of Mathematics*, 2d ed. p. 338 (Macmillan, 1893).

63 This work appeared in 1738, based on a draft apparently written six or seven years prior to that. Bernoulli, Nicolas; letter of 5 April 1732, acknowledging that he received "Specimen theoriae novae metiendi sortem pecuniariam."

64 Bernoulli, Daniel; "Specimen theoriae novae de mensura sortis" in Commentarii Academiae Scientiarum Imperialis Petropolitanae 5 (1738); reprinted in translation as "Exposition of a new theory on the measurement of risk" in Econometrica 22 (1954). (Bernoulli's lasting claim to fame is that his study of fluid dynamics led to the "Bernoulli effect" which in turn explains how airplanes get their lift and sails their force.)

65 See http://en.wikipedia.org/wiki/St._Petersburg_paradox. This fascinated Bernoulli and Cramer. The paradox involves a theoretical lottery that leads to a random variable that at once offers an infinite expected payoff and at the same time would be worth only trivial money. Footnote 22: the article that you cite in 20 includes Bernoulli's logarithm and briefly discusses Cramer on page 33. The cite for the Econometrica reprint is. Bernoulli, Daniel, Exposition of a New Theory on the Measurement of Risk, Econometrica, Vol. 22, No. 1)Jan., 1954), pp. 23, 36. The logarithm starts on page 26. Preinreich, Gabriel A.D., Progressive Taxation and Proportionate Sacrifice, The American Economic Review, Vol. 38, No. 1

conclusions as to the mathematical rate of decline in the value of money.[66] Unfortunately, their thinking had only a brief moment in the sun.

The next participant of note is Adam Smith (1723-1790) who in 1776 made a famous remark about taxation that reflected the concept of the declining marginal utility of money. It appears in Book IV of the *Wealth of Nations*:[67]

> "The necessaries of life occasion the great expense of the poor. They find it difficult to get food, and the greater part of their little revenue is spent in getting it. The luxuries and vanities of life occasion the principal expense of the rich, and a magnificent house embellishes and sets off to the best advantage all the other luxuries and vanities which they possess. A tax upon house-rents, therefore, would in general fall heaviest upon the rich; and in this sort of inequality there would not, perhaps, be anything very unreasonable. It is not very unreasonable that the rich should contribute to the public expense, not only in proportion to their revenue, but something more than in that proportion."[68]

Smith considered that as a practical matter taxes on income would create distortions in behavior and preferred taxes on wealth in the form of land because such were administrable and because if wealth taxes were extended to commodities, they would lead to inflation and collusion.[69] He saw property rights as a necessity for any government and believed that successful economies would be characterized by governments that protect the rich from the envious poor. His proposal was for a wealth

(Mar., 1948), pp. 103-117. Footnote 9 on Page 111 states, "Cramer's thought was that pleasure afforded by wealth increases as the square root of its amount. This means u = ½." The footnote also discusses Bernoulli, whose logarithm is discussed in the paper on pg. 111.

Shoemaker, Paul J. H., The Expected Utility Model; Its Variants, Purposes, Evidence and Limitations, Journal of Economic Literature, Vol. 20, No. 2 (Jun., 1982) pp. 529-63. This work briefly discusses Cramer and Bernoulli on pp. 530-31 and discusses the fact that Bernoulli used a logarithm. Friedman, Milton and Savage, L.J., The Utility Analysis of Choices Involving Risk, Journal of Political Economy, Vol. 56, No. 4 (Aug., 1948) pp. 279-304. Footnote 5 on pg. 281 of this work discusses Bernoulli and Cramer, and the fact that Bernoulli is generally given credit for this idea because he came up with the logarithm, but it does not mention exactly the formula Cramer used.

66 Cramer selected a square root. Preinreich, Gabriel A.D., Progressive Taxation and Proportionate Sacrifice, The American Economic Review, Vol. 38, No. 1 (Mar., 1948), pp. 111 (footnote 9).

67 Adam Smith, An Inquiry into the Nature And Causes of the Wealth of Nations (1776). Book Five: Of the Revenue of the Sovereign or Commonwealth. CHAPTER II: Of the Sources of the General or Public Revenue of the Society. ARTICLE I: Taxes upon the Rent of House.

68 Id. Book IV, Of the Revenue of the Sovereign or Commonwealth.

69 Adam Smith, 5 LECTURES ON JURISPRUDENCE (R. L. Meek, D. D. Raphael & P. G. Stein eds., Glasgow Edition of the Works And Correspondence of Adam Smith, Oxford: Clarendon Press 1976)

tax with a large exemption and a flat rate was in part in order to achieve progressivity of rates.[70]

Jeremy Bentham made by far the greater contribution. He was a rare genius who graduated from Oxford at 15 and became a lawyer, dedicating his life to numerous reforms, including animal rights. He echoed Aristotle's observation about the declining utility of money and applied a great deal of effort to formalizing the subject. The following famous passage offers his thoughts on the taxation of wealth, but it is equally applicable to the taxation of income:

> "Of two people having unequal fortunes, he who has most wealth must by a legislator be regarded as having most happiness. But the quantity of happiness will not go on increasing in anything near the same proportion as the quantity of wealth: ten thousand times the quantity of wealth will not bring with it ten thousand times the quantity of happiness. It will even be matter of doubt, whether ten thousand times the wealth will in general bring with it twice the happiness. Thus it is, that, the effect of wealth in the production of happiness goes on diminishing, as the quantity by which the wealth of one man exceeds that of another goes on increasing: In other words, the quantity of happiness produced by a particle of wealth (each particle being of the same magnitude) will be less and less at every particle; the second will produce less than the first, the third than the second, and so on."[71]

Bentham and John Stuart Mill – who are often referred to in the same breath -- are considered to have founded the school of economic philosophy known as Consequentialism, a forerunner of Utilitarianism, which is itself the foundation for modern microeconomics and is in turn the basis for much serious Congressional testimony by economists. The heart of their doctrine is that the merits or flaws of human actions ought to be judged by the pleasure or pain that they imply for the population and not by abstract normative measures.[72]

Bentham's thoughts are profound because they call for considering not only dryly logical matters of consumption and production, but also the distributive effects of policy choices in the realm of taxation and economics. His search might be called the quest for maximizing aggregate national happiness (or "utility") considering all the participants,

---

[70] Id., *See also* Beverly I. Moran, *Capitalism and the Tax System: A Search For Social Justice,* 61 SMU L. Rev. 337, 343-47 (2008).

[71] Bentham, Jeremy, and Browring, Sir John, The Works Of Jeremy Bentham, Volume 3, pp. 228-29 (W. Tait, 1843)

[72] For an excellent, short discussion of this subject and much more, see Uwe Reinhart, *How Economists Bastardized Benthamite Utilitarianism,* which can be found at ^http://www.princeton.edu/~reinhard/pdfs/100-Next_How_Economists_Bastardized_Benthamite_Utilitarianism.pdf

which in its modern form is often described inaccurately as the search for "the greatest good for the greatest number." He referred to the effort to value the results of an act, whether positive or negative, as the *felicific calculus*. The theory is spectacularly powerful, but its applications can be exasperating. Not only is it hard to assign values to acts, but there is also the formal problem that not every similarly situated person assigns the same value to anything. The modern evolution of this effort is the study of welfare economics, which searches for aggregate gains known as "social surplus" via changes in public policy. An important related principle states that if a new policy results in a net financial gain to society then the losers ought to be rewarded with a lump sum payment.[73] For example, if one were to impose a tax on a very useful toxin in order to discourage its production and consumption, one might make compensatory payments to poor consumers, who would then be free to decide whether to use the money to buy the same toxic product or put the money to better uses. This is taken up again later in the article.

Bentham is viewed as favoring taxes on wealth over taxes on labor. He famously said, "Most taxes are, as all taxes ought to be, taxes upon affluence."[74]

John Stuart Mill's thoughts were at once more conservative and more radical. His preference was for proportional taxes on earned income in order to encourage personal exertion, provided that poorer people's necessities were not threatened. He considered designing progressive income taxes an impossible task for the legislature. As to gratuitous transfers, however, graduated rates were desirable and his views would likely be considered surprisingly ruthless today:

> "With respect to the large fortunes acquired by gift or inheritance, the power of bequeathing is one of those privileges of property which are fit subjects for regulation on grounds of general expediency; and I have already suggested, as a possible mode of restraining the accumulation of large fortunes in the hands of those who have not earned them by exertion, a limitation of the amount which any one person should be permitted to acquire by gift, bequest, or inheritance. Apart from this, and from the proposal of Bentham (also discussed in a former chapter) that collateral inheritance in case of intestacy should cease, and the property escheat to the state, I conceive that inheritances and legacies, exceeding a certain amount, are highly proper subjects for taxation: and that the revenue from them should be as great as it can be made without giving rise to evasions,

---

73 See, e.g., S.Jain & S. Makunda, Economic Policy Reform under Political Constraints: Labor Reallocation and Compensatory Redistribution, draft of presentation at 2003 NEUDC conference, Yale University (September 2003), available at http://aida.econ.yale.edu/conference/neudc03/papers/8e-jain.pdf.

74 Jeremy Bentham, the Works of Jeremy Bentham, The Online Library of Liberty, .p. 1033, a project of Liberty Fund, Inc. available at:
http://files.libertyfund.org/pll/pdf/Bentham_0872-02_EBk_v6.0.pdf.

> by donation during life or concealment of property, such as it would be impossible adequately to check. The principle of graduation (as it is called,) that is, of levying a larger percentage on a larger sum, though its application to general taxation would be in my opinion objectionable, seems to me both just and expedient as applied to legacy and inheritance duties.[75]

Mill at least initially opposed progressive income taxation on the ground that it violated "equality of sacrifice" and penalized people who work hard and save and therefore constituted "a mild form of robbery," but as we have seen did not feel the same way about taking unearned income or inherited wealth.

There are occasional examples of this thinking in American tax law. During the Nixon Administration top federal income tax rates on unearned income were 70 percent, but 50 percent on earned income and the legislative history of the estate tax contained an explicit intention to break up great wealth.[76]

Marginal utility theory – the heart of microeconomics -- took strong hold in the early Nineteenth Century in the hands of such people as William Lloyd (1795/1852), who propounded a form of general utility theory[77] as did Hermann Gossen (1810/1858).[78] Marginal utility refers to the gain from adding an extra unit of a good or service or loss from a decrease in the consumption of the good or service. Its common application is the "law of diminishing returns" under which as a consumer acquires each further unit of the good or service, his or her enjoyment (utility) declines in comparison to the prior unit.

James Madison, the American Revolution and the Importance of Civic Virtue

There is a strain in the early history of the United States that is rarely appreciated or taken seriously, namely the notion of civic virtue. It t stands as a forgotten counterpoint to our modern combative political environment and this country's frequent

[75] J. S, Mill, Principles Of Political Economy With Some Of Their Applications To Social Philosophy (Longman, Greens &Co. 1878)., p. 487.

[76] Recently restated in S. REP. NO. 144, 97th Cong., 1st Sess. 124, reprinted in 1981 U.S. CODE CONG. & AD. NEWS 105, 226 ("Historically, one of the principal reasons for estate and gift taxes was to break up large concentrations of wealth") This claim has been repudiated as mere myth. See Michael Graetz, To Praise the Estate Tax, Not to Bury It, 93 Yale L.J. 259 (1983) (estate tax a s supplement to progressivity).

[77] A Lecture on the Notion of Value as Distinguished Not Only from Utility, but also from Value in Exchange, forming part of his Lectures on Population, Value, Poor Laws and Rent (1837).[34]

[78] Die Entwicklung der Gesetze des menschlichen Verkehrs und der daraus fließenden Regeln für menschliches Handeln (1854). The book is heavily mathematical. The book has been translated into English under the title The Laws of Human Relations and the Rules of Human Action Derived Therefrom (MIT Press 1983).

subordination of moral philosophy by materialistic political rhetoric. Utilitarianism was not part of the American thread of virtuous citizenship, but at the same time, Utilitarianism drew much of its strength from ancient concepts of virtue.[79]

The intellectual history of the founding of the United States found inspiration in England's "Country Party" whose ideology referred back to visions of the Greek *polis* and Roman republic, both of which were seen as free of greed and corruption, run by a virtuous populace.[80] Indeed, there was evidently a widespread belief that America was a fresh blessing from God, which buttressed the social importance of banishing corruption.[81] At the same time there was an inevitable paradox; the Constitution secured property rights and created freedom of commerce, which could lead to the ascendancy of greed and venality. John Quincy Adams once summarized the dilemma this way in a private letter:

> "Public Virtue cannot exist without private, and public Virtue is the only Foundation of Republics. There must be a positive Passion for the public good, the public Interest, Honor, Power, and Glory, established in the Minds of the People, or there can be no Republican Government, nor any real Liberty. And this public Passion must be Superior to all private Passions. Men must be ready, they must pride themselves, and be happy to sacrifice their private Pleasures, Passions, and Interests, nay their private Friendships and dearest connections, when they Stand in Competition with the Rights of society."[82]

He feared "a great Danger that a Republican Government would be very factious and turbulent . . ."[83] After the Revolution, faith in civic virtue as sufficient had declined, there was a general recognition that people are not always virtuous, and that there was a risk of tyrannical government, to which Madison (who drew on Artistotle's *Politics*[84]) recommended modified a Constitution based on gridlock ("divided powers") whereby an internally restricted government would expend much its energy fighting itself, thereby

79 For a general discussion see G. Edward White, The Political Economy of The Original Constitution, 35 Harv. J.L. & Pub. Pol'y 61
(Winter, 2012). The subject is Capitalism, Markets, and the Constitution The Thirtieth Annual Federalist Society National Student Symposium on Law and Public Policy--2011 II. Economic Theory, Civic Virtue, and the Meaning of the Constitution G. Edward White

80 H. T. Dickinson, ed., A companion to eighteenth-century Britain (2002) p. 30. See also J.G.A. Pocock, The Machiavellian Moment p 507.

81 Bernard Bailyn, The Ideological Origins of the American Revolution p 525.

82 Letter to Mercy Otis Warren (1776), from Paul Rahe, Republics Ancient and Modern: Classical Republicanism and the American Revolution. Volume: II, p. 23. (North Carolina Press 1994).

83 Id. .

84 Colleen A. Sheehan, James Madison and the Spirit of Republican Self-Government, (Cambridge University Press, 2009) pp.161-163. (especially with respect to stability of regimes).

posing less of a threat to liberty.[85] Madison also foresaw the risk that private interests that might come to dominate government and subvert the public good and the risk of "faction," meaning self-interested groups such as landowners and merchants, debtors and creditors and hence saw the need for public education in civics.[86] In Federalist No. 10, he argued that it was impossible to control factions without unduly infringing on personal liberty and recommended ways to design government to minimize their mischief. In the end, his model prevailed.

Things are never as simple as they may seem. Madison's mechanical design of government still presupposed civic virtue, which nowadays seems almost quaint. Here is his presupposition:

> "But I go on this great republican principle, that the people will have virtue and intelligence to select men of virtue and wisdom. Is there no virtue among us? If there be not, we are in a wretched situation. No theoretical checks, no form of government, can render us secure . . ."[87]

Madison considered we were safe as long as a virtuous citizenry selected its leaders:

> "If there be sufficient virtue and intelligence in the community, it will be exercised in the selection of these men [representatives of the people]; so that we do not depend on their virtue, or put confidence in our rulers, but in the people who are to choose them. "[88]

If one agrees with Madison, this raises the disturbing question of whether serious discussions of progressive taxation can occur in an environment in which the citizenry has lost faith in its politicians and lobbyists and Washington insiders who can provide desperately needed campaign funds to influence the agenda.

The American Civil War

---

85 See generally Gordon S. Wood, The Radicalism of the American Revolution ____ (1992). Hamilton feared business forces and landowner forces with excessive representation in legislatures. The Federalist No. 35, at 214-16 (Alexander Hamilton) (Clinton Rossiter ed., 1961).
Hamilton also believed the public would select wise, disinterested legislators. Id. at 214-16

86 So did Thomas Jefferson, among others. Akhil R. Amar, The Bill of Rights: Creation and Reconstruction 131-33 (Yale U. Press 1998).

87 James Madison, Remarks to the Virginia Convention, in Vol. 3, The Debates in the Several State Conventions on the Adoption of the Federal Constitution, 536-537 (Jonathan Elliot, Ed. 2d Ed. 1836).

88 Madison, James, and Ketcham, Ralph Louis, Selected Writings of James Madison 157-58 (Hackett Publishing Company, Inc. 2006) and originally from Virginia Convention Speech, June 20, 1788.

Prior the Civil War the nation depended mainly on import duties to fund the federal government. In addition, there were occasional excise taxes that the government imposed temporarily when customs revenues were inadequate (e.g., to fund the War of 1812), along with revenues from the sale of public lands.[89] The first American progressive income tax was enacted by the Union in the Revenue Act of 1862, long after the formulation of utility theory in economics, but with no evidence visible to this writer that utility theory ever crept into the debate. The tax was levied on individuals; if income exceeded $600 but not $10,000, individuals were taxed at 3%; if income exceeded $10,000, individuals were taxed at 5%.[90] So it was a progressive income tax, presumably founded on simple notions of fairness and political expediency.

The legislative history is dissatisfying. Congressional floor debates are typically useful when examining the policies Congress takes into account before enacting tax legislation, however, the *Congressional Record*, which now collects and sanitizes Congressional floor debates, did not exist until 1873, long after the tax was enacted.[91] As a result, to obtain insight into Congressional considerations regarding the Revenue Act of 1862, one has to examine the *Congressional Globe*, a newspaper-like collation of pre-1873 Congressional deliberations.[92] Because the *Globe* did not provide verbatim accounts, as does the *Record*,[93] but instead provided rough outlines of the debates, and because the *Globe* was thought to be partisan, with certain members misrepresented or not represented at all, the information regarding Congress' reasoning for instituting a progressive tax is lacking.[94]

Nonetheless, the *Congressional Globe* does provide a snapshot of the post-Civil War era in America that helps understand what Congressmen took into consideration before enacting a progressive tax system. The Revenue Act of 1862 was seen largely as a wartime emergency measure, enacted to meet the Union's increased financial demands arising from the conflict with the Confederacy.[95] Aside from the exigencies of war expenditures, the Union had relied on various tax revenues from the southern States before enacting the new progressive tax. Congressmen considered the tax as a means to recoup such losses as import taxes[96] or taxes on slavery.[97] Be that as it may, there is no

89 B. Bittker & L. Lokken, FEDERAL TAXATION OF INCOME, ESTATES AND GIFTS, ¶1.1.2. (WG&L, supplemented through 2012).

90 Revenue Act of 1862, Sec. 90, 12 Stat. 432, at 473 (July 1, 1862).

91 Richard J. McKinney, An overview of the Congressional Record and Its Predecessor Publications: A Research Guide, LAW LIBRARIAN'S SOCIETY OF WASHINGTON, D.C., October 2011. Available at http://www.llsdc.org/cong-record/

92 Id.

93 Nowadays the language is in fact sanitized before the Congressional Record is printed.

94 Elizabeth G. McPherson, Reporting the Debates of Congress, 28 QUAR. J. SPEECH 145-146 (1942).

95 Report of the Secretary of Treasury on the Sate of Finances, WASHINGTON: GOVERNMENT PRINTING OFFICE, 6, 126-7, (1863)

96 THE CONGRESSIONAL GLOBE, JANUARY 18, 450-459, (1862)

97 THE CONGRESSIONAL GLOBE, MAY 29, 442-443 (1862)

evidence of philosophical reasoning behind the progressivity of the tax rates. There is certainly no reference to Utilitarian thought.

The 16th Amendment and Revenue Act of 1913

The Revenue Act of 1913 was America's first modern, durable progressive tax.[98] It went into force following the ratification of the Sixteenth Amendment to the United States Constitution, which made Constitutional the collection of taxes from "whatever source derived."[99] By today's standards the rates were modest.

> "In addition to the income tax provided under this section (herein referred to as the normal income tax) there shall be levied, assessed, and collected upon the net income of every individual an additional income tax (herein referred to as the additional tax) 1 per centum per annum upon the amount by which the total net income exceeds $20,000 and does not exceed $50,000, and 2 per centum per annum upon the amount by which the total net income exceeds $50,000 and does not exceed $75,000, 3 per centum per annum upon the amount by which the total net income exceeds $75,000 and does not exceed $100,000, 4 per centum per annum upon the amount by which the total net income exceeds $100,000 and does not exceed $250,000, 5 per centum per annum upon the amount by which the total net income exceeds $250,000 and does not exceed $500,000, and 6 per centum per annum upon the amount by which the total net income exceeds $500,000."[100]

In order to shift some of the financial burden from those least able to bear it onto the shoulders of the wealthy, the Revenue Act offset high tariffs with a progressive income

---

98 Both the North and the South briefly enacted income taxes during the Civil War. The South imposed multiple taxes which included an 8% tax on naval stores and agricultural products, a 1% tax on the value of securities and invested capital in businesses and a series of licenses on trades, businesses and occupations, some of which were based on gross receipts. Additionally, a tax on salaries and a tax on income and profits were levied.
See William D. Samson, *The Nineteenth Century Income Tax in the South,* 12 Accounting Historians J., S No.1, (Spring 1985). The North's was "progressive" in that it initially levied a tax of 3 percent on annual incomes over $600 but less than $10,000 and a tax of 5 percent above that level. Cynthia G. Fox, *Income Tax Records of the Civil War Years*, 18 Prologue, No. 4 (1986).

99 The Amendment was necessary to bypass the Supreme Court's invalidation of a prior tax on Constitutional grounds, primarily that as applied to dividends, interest, and other income from personal property, it was a "direct" tax which requiring the burden to be apportioned among the States in proportion to their populations, a Herculean requirement. Pollock v. Farmers' Loan & Trust Co., 157 US 429, 158 US 601 (1895).

100 REVENUE ACT OF 1913, Section II, A.2., 38 Stat. 114, 166

tax that effectively largely exempted the poorest Americans. Again, a look at the Congressional debates from the period leading up to the 1913 Act provides an insight into the reasoning behind implementing a progressive income tax scheme. Congressmen of the day considered both social fairness and, implicitly, Utilitarianism.

> "It is a shame and a disgrace, Mr. Speaker, that under our system of taxation the poor laboring man who has a wife and four or five children to support contributes more toward the expenses of the Government than does the millionaire who is too proud to raise a family and has no one to clothe and feed except a wife and a poodle dog... [Polarization of wealth] affects injuriously every citizen, unless it be the few who fatten at the expense of the many."[101]

> "Any Tariff measure which would mean the greatest good for the greatest number would receive my support [shades of Bentham here]. I would endeavor in every measure to ascertain whether it [the Act] would promote the public welfare, weaken special privilege, and help to give every man a fair and square chance before supporting it... I believe that this bill is more just than the present law to the people of the Nation, that as a whole it will improve conditions and bring more of justice and less of oppression to the common man."[102]

Congressmen also considered the argument that taxes on individuals with higher incomes tend to fall much more on economic rent[103] than taxes on those with low incomes:

> "Under the indirect taxes which people have been paying heretofore, which have been largely consumption taxes – because the poor consume out of all proportion to their income of what the rich consume as to their income – the men of small means and small incomes have been paying an extraordinarily large share of the taxes to support the government."[104]

The striking omission in these early revenue acts is the absence of a discussion of why the rates were set at progressive levels and why the particular breakpoints between rates

101 Congressional Record Bound, CR-1909-0712, 4434 (1909)

102 Congressional Record Bound, CR-1913-0506, 1251 (1913)

103 Rent is an economic term referring to the difference between what a factor of production (i.e., capital, land, or labor) earns and what it could earn in the next best-paid employment. It is generally thought of pejoratively in the sense that a competitive, efficient market would squeeze out rent and offer only "normal" returns. Rent is often considered a fair target of taxation because it can be appropriated without negative effects on consumption and production. See, e.g., Tollison, "Rent Seeking: A Survey" Kyklos, vol. 35, issue 4, pp. 575-602 (1982).

104 Id., at 1250.

were selected. Instead, we see *faits accomplis* which we can only attribute to political compromise and private intuitions of legislators.

America in the Twenty-First Century

Americans pride themselves on their energy, optimism and entrepreneurship and tend to look at increases in the Gross Domestic Product as the measure of national economic success. As a result of this context, arguments about appropriate levels of taxation are generally couched in terms of economic outcomes, with "fairness" generally conceived as an ideological preference. The guiding principle of maximizing production and consumption has tilted the discussion into materialistic realms characterized by bitter forensics and deep questions about whether the debate itself is tainted by an undue influence of money in politics and rigid ideologies on all sides.

The "Right" Level of Progressivity

This subject could not be more controversial and incapable of a precise conclusion. The debate largely turns on intuitive notions of fairness and what is best for the overall economy rather than on morality or the coherent approach of Utilitarianism.[105] What follows are a few of the common arguments and considerations concerning changes in top federal income tax rates.

The "Substitution" and "Income Effects"

Perhaps the most common argument is that progressive taxes are inherently imprudent because they cause productive people to withdraw their labor (the "substitution effect").[106] A completely contradictory and offsetting theory proposes that progression does no harm because heavily taxed individuals will work harder in order to maintain their prior standard of living (the "income effect"). As always in the American tax realm, the empirical evidence is not satisfying because it is sparse and dated, but at least there is some. Unfortunately, this line of honest inquiry died out decades ago. Although it generally favors the income effect over the substitution effect, ideologues seems blissfully unaware of its existence.

---

105 The legal and economic literature in this field is exceptionally voluminous. Perhaps the most comprehensive survey is by Bankman and Griffith, *Social Welfare and the Rate Structure: A new Look at Progressive Taxation*, 75 Cal. L. Rev. 1095 (1984).

106 See B. Bittker & L. Lokken, Federal Taxation of Income Estates & Gifts ¶ 3.2 (Warren, Gorham & Lamont 2011).

The first empirical study appeared during the Great Depression and was authored by Professor Paul Douglas, who later became Senator Douglas of Illinois.[107] The upshot of his study was that reducing wages generally makes people work longer.[108] This implies that rising tax rates would be met with more work, not less, and supports the income effect, especially in the case of the young, the old and females. This study and its implications are summarized neatly as follows:

> "These results comport with a common sense analysis: Since most middle-aged men already work full-time, they could not readily increase their earnings to offset higher taxes. On the other hand, when the primary breadwinner's take-home pay is reduced by taxation, one would expect high school students, retired persons, and housewives to give up their unpaid activities and seek gainful employment in order to restore the status quo ante."[109]

Later studies validated Douglas' conclusions, showing that a reduction in the wages of middle-aged wives drove them to leave the work force, and a variety of other results, all of which were dependent on the socio-cultural patterns of those earlier times, especially the greater prevalence of the husband as the primary breadwinner.[110]

> "Efforts have been made to measure the impact of income taxes on the choice between work and leisure not only by statistical studies but also by questionnaires. When asked about the effect of taxes on their work habits, an overwhelming majority of wage earners, salaried employees, and self-employed professionals deny that the impact is substantial."[111]

To make it even more complicated, one can take into account how taxes are spent; if the

---

107 Douglas had a remarkable career. He taught at the University of Chicago, served on the Chicago City Council and was a marine in WWII, leaving as lieutenant colonel and war hero.

108 Douglas, The Theory of Wages 313 (Kelley & Millman, Inc. 1934); see Break, The Incidence and Economic Effects of Taxation, in Economics of Public Finance 187 (Blinder & Solow eds., Brookings 1984).

109 B. Bittker & L.Lokken, Federal Taxation of Income, Estates and Gifts, ¶ 3.2 (WG&L supplemented through 2012).

110 Id,, citing inter alia Boskin, The Economics of Labor Supply, in Income Maintenance and Labor Supply 163–181 (Cain & Watts eds., Academic Press 1973) and Kosters, Effects of an Income Tax on Labor Supply, in The Taxation of Income From Capital (Harberger & Bailey eds., Brookings 1969).

111 Id., citing inter alia Barlow, Brazer & Morgan, Economic Behavior of the Affluent 129–150 (Brookings 1966); Brown & Levin, The Effects of Income Taxation on Overtime: The Results of a National Survey, 84 Econ. J. 833 (1974); Fields & Stanbury, Income Taxes and Incentives to Work, 61 Am. Econ. Rev. 435 (1971); Holland, The Effect of Taxation on Effort: Some Results for Business Executives, 62 Proc. Nat'l Tax Ass'n 428 (1969).

spending favors the poor and middle class, then the degree of progressivity increases.[112] Plato did not do so in *Laws*, presumably because he felt the moral imperative behind the system of taxation and distribution of taxes regulated both components and viewed the sum of the two as the correct measure. Our debates are far more raucous, and we seem unable to agree on what is fair on either the tax or spending side and depend on intuition rather than scrupulous analysis of the seemingly ideological claims. That is not to say that the government's failure to study the impact of changes in tax rates is abnormal. In reality, such studies are all but nonexistent in all areas of income taxation where matters are settled by forensics and lobbying and then often left for the next administration to grapple with.

The belittling of Utilitarian thought

Bentham and Mill's[113] Utilitarian views are potentially revolutionary if one combines the utilities to be gained from income taxation plus redistribution of that income. The obvious implication is a reduction of economic inequalities, and, if pushed far enough, socialism and ultimately even equality. Microeconomics dominates the academic debate over progressive income taxation, but game theory and behavioral economics seem to be rapidly displacing the study of microeconomics.[114] Although microeconomics itself was born from Utilitarian principles and freely uses "utility" as a crucial tool of analysis, in this author's view it has been largely sterilized because of economists' dread of making "normative" statements. To frame the question, one can consider the following example.[115]

> **To Illustrate:** Islandia has 2 citizens, R (rich) and P (poor). R has 100 pies of income this year and P has three. The pies are necessary to the operation of the government and have no redistributive implications. The economists in Islandia and elsewhere agree there is a declining marginal utility of money. A flat wealth tax rate tax of 10% would cause P to suffer but would be emotionally trivial to R. Intuitively (viewed from abroad) it would be fairer to not tax P and to present R

---

112 R. Musgrave & P. Musgrave, Public Finance in Theory and Practice 261-65 (4th ed. 1984).

113 Mills was leery about progressive income taxation of the fruits of labor. Interestingly, in the US tax rates declined in stages in which income from labor was preferred over income from capital, sharing Mills' preference. Specifically, The top individual rate was 90 percent at the end of WWII, then 70 percent in 1964, then 50 percent for earned income in 1969, then 50 percent for all income in 1981.

114 John Von Neumann & Oskar Morgenstern, Theory of Games and Economic Behavior (1944) is the starting point, and the application of game theory to economics began in earnest with the work of John C. Harsanyi, *Games with Incomplete Information Played by "Bayesian" Players*, 14 Mgmt. Sci. 159-182, 320-334, 486-502 (1967-1968), Modern treatments of industrial organization commonly include game theory. See, e.g., Dennis Carlton & Jeffrey Perloff, Modern Industrial Organization (2000).

115 This example can be faulted for incompleteness. Are the taxes somehow avoidable? Are they one shot or do they run into the indefinite future, etc.? These issues are not trivial, but are dismissed for purposes of framing the question in a stark light.

with a tax bill of three pies.

Microeconomists have various objections to the intuitive solution.

There is no proper definition of utility. This is a legitimate complaint. Bentham defined utility modestly in terms of a:

> " . . . hedonistic calculus: in comparing two actions under consideration, we count up the pleasures or pains each will produce . . . then sum them up for all persons who will be affected. Evidently these directions can at best produce only approximate results."[116]

Exactly how to measure individual utility has become a confused subject.[117] Not even Bentham and Mill agreed on how to define utility. In terms of P and R, how do we measure the impact of the proposed tax?

Mill's method has been called "Rule Utilitarian" because he considered utility had to be confined by morality. For example, one taxpayer's not paying her taxes would bring greater utility to her, but would be catastrophic if no one paid any tax.

> "Mill therefore seems to appeal to a second type of rule-utilitarian theory, one that does not evaluate moral rules in comparative isolation, as in utilitarian generalization, but rather considers them as component parts of a more complex *ideal moral code*, a set of rules that together *would* maximize utility if it was adopted and followed by the overwhelming majority of the members of a society."[118]

This harks back to the Ancients in that it is concerned with moral virtue as the first principle. So much for the idea that hedonism reigns supreme in Utilitarian thought.

In the next stage, Victorian economists adopted Bentham's ideas of presumed pleasure and pain as the measure of utility, but not for long:

> "[O]nce economists discovered (in the "marginalist revolution" of the early part of the twentieth century) that they did not need to attribute utility functions to economic agents in order to prove most of the propositions that seemed

[116] The Cambridge Dictionary of Philosophy, p. 69 (Audi, Ed., Cambridge Univ. Press 1995).

[117] I have relied heavily on a paper by Ken Binmore entitled "Interpersonal Comparison of Utility" for this topic. He is a member of the Economics Department University of London. Ken Binmore, Interpersonal Comparison of Utility, in Kincaid & Ross (eds.) *Oxford Handbook of Philosophy of Economic Science*, (Oxford University Press 2009)

[118] Henry R. West, Blackwell's Guide to Mill's Utilitarianism, pp. 144-145 (Blackwell Pub. Ltd.2006)

> important at the time, all of the baggage on utility theory inherited from the Victorian era was swept away."[119]

Modern theory moved away from explaining people's behavior in favor of observing their behavior objectively; this observed behavior is known as "revealed preferences.[120] Leading thinkers in this sphere are Von Neumann and Morgenstern who came up with an imaginative way to determine people's utility scale for money by reference to lotteries, but it does not solve the matter of interpersonal comparisons.[121] This is the next topic.

Each person's utility varies. This raises the matter of "interpersonal comparisons." It might be that R enjoys giving away his money and that P finds living near the starvation level to be exciting. There is an illuminating example of differing preferences from the Enlightenment philosopher David Hume:[122]

"Were I Alexander," said Parmenio, "I would accept these offers made by Darius."

"So would I too," replied Alexander, "were I Parmenio."

The topic of how to isolate, rank and value individual preferences brings one into extremely deep and uncertain waters. Whatever those preferences are, they are shaped by societal factors that are themselves in motion. It seems possible to identify a best method,[123] but actually applying it to concrete proposals for tax legislation is impossible.

There was a time when there was a view that because one cannot accurately determine people's specific utilities, the defect was so severe that it presented a serious case for discarding utility theory.[124] This theory lives on as a bugaboo in the literature of microeconomics and raises exasperating questions that are ultimately all but impossible to apply scientifically in connection with the making of tax policy. A good example of

---

119 Binmore, p. 3.

120 Binmore p.4.

121 See Ken Binmore, Rational Decisions 58-59 (2009) for a critique.

122 David Hume, *An enquiry concerning the principles of morals*, pg. 146, (London, 1751).

123 Bimore's erudiate article proposes that Harsanyi's is the best. See J. Harsanyi, Normative Validity and Meaning of Von Neumann and Morgensern Utilities, in B. Skyrms, ed., Studies in Logic and the Foundations of Game Theory: Proceedings of the Ninth International Congress Of Logic, Methodology And The Philosophy Of Science (Kluwer 1992); Binmore at pp. 15-17.

124 The best known example of this attitude appears in Blum & Klaven, *The Uneasy Case for Progressive Taxation.*, 19 U. Chi. L. Rev. 417 (1952). Blum and Kalvin's analysis is schizophrenic in that it rejects the utilitarian approach overall, but confesses that welfare considerations are legitimate when one compares the tax burden on two individuals, one of whose income is below subsistence and the other has an income above the subsistence level. Id. at 473. Common sense suggests this is merely the most compelling case, not the only case.

impossible quests in the field of economics is the "right tax" to impose on petroleum in order to account for the implicit damage each unit of petroleum does. A great deal of ink has been spent on the subject, and there is simply no single correct answer because the necessary information is lacking.[125]

Despite the impossibility of achieving perfection, and the arguable uselessness of microeconomics to solve the problem of just how to calibrate a set of income tax rates, utilitarian thought is so stubbornly embedded in economic theory that it will stubbornly remain with us, primarily as a basis for looking at proposals for changed tax rates. At the same time, economists decline to opine on the collective social utility of taxes because they consider it is not their charge, although they have formalized the subject of maximizing overall utility in a narrow way, and although various mathematically inclined economists have presented their theorems under the rubric of the "social welfare function," often with intricate graphs and symbolic logic.[126]

Modern Economists and Testimony on Inefficiency

In a country much taken with free-market ideology such as ours, economists' testimony that a proposed change in the tax laws will be "inefficient" sounds grave, but what are they saying exactly in their language? Efficiency means an adjustment in the allocation of resources within society results in at least one person feeling better off and none feeling worse off[127], an idea within the sphere of welfare economics which is a descendant of Utilitarianism. If they are scrupulous they will stop at identifying the winners and losers and quantify the impacts if possible, and leave the policy decision concerning the social merit of proposed legislation to the legislators; this is known as "strict constructionism" among economists.[128]

The trouble is, there are apt to be losers and the data presented by economists frequently depend on the economists' claims as to what the correct inputs are. Proposals for taxes on environmental "bads," such as CO2 emissions offer an excellent example of vast

125 For one point of entry on this impossible topic see M. Walls, Welfare Costs On An Oil Import Fee, 8-2 Contemporary Economic Policy, pp. 176-189 (1990) (opposing view of desirability of oil tax).

126 See, e.g., Anthony Atkinson & Joseph Stieligtz, Lectures on Public Economics (McGraw Hill 1980) pp. 339- 340 and Samuel Bowles, Microeconomics: Behavior, Institutions, and Evolutions, p.p. 221-227 (2004). See also, Bankman & Griffith, Social Welfare and the Rate Structure: A New Look at Progressive Taxation, 75 Calif. L. Rev. 1905 (1987); Byrne, Locke, Property, and Progressive Taxes, 78 Neb. L. Rev. 700 (1999).

127 This is known as a "Pareto optimum" after the Italian economist Vilfredo Pareto (1848–1923) and is commonly used as a guide for fashioning economic policies.

128 See William J. Baumol, Welfare Economics and the Theory of the State, (Harvard U. Press 1965)

disagreements.[129] It is naïve to think that personal preferences (and sometimes funding from private parties) do not creep into the analyses.

In addition, assuming a policy proposal is not "efficient" in the highly restricted sense that at least one person is worse off as a result of a change, economists will commonly propose that the winners compensate the losers with lump-sum taxes (a one-shot tax of set amount of money per victim). [130] If after the new tax plus the compensation the winners are all better off, then under this analysis overall social welfare increases and the policy is a good one. This approach allows an escape from the rigor of strict constructionism. The trouble is that while this is fine in theory compensation is extremely difficult to implement, yet the policy is apt to be approved anyway.[131] Putting that aside, economists will testify that there will be inefficiencies, commonly expressed as "deadweight losses." However, it is much easier to testify that there is an inefficiency than to calculate it. One remedy is to expand the economists' mandate to include quantifying the inefficiency, after which the policy makers can better evaluate the choices the proposal represents,[132] but scrupulous economists are apt to decline the invitation, considering it an offer of a fool's errand.

The modern rhetorical objections to progressive taxation

Opponents of progressive taxation have busied themselves with economic criticisms. What follows is a description of the principal objections and the common proposal for an alternative system. What they have in common is that they are all based on materialistic considerations.

Inefficiency and deadweight loss . The discussion of economic efficiency in the formal sense as used in welfare analysis has been discussed above, but there are numerous other objections that rely on "inefficiency" to repudiate proposed increases in tax rates on the high end of the economic income ladder. In this contention sphere there are at least four different variations of "inefficiency," namely (1) resources wasted in adjusting to transitions in the tax laws, (2) tax laws that unintentionally distort behavior compared to a situation, free of taxes (3) unduly intricate laws, and (4) high tax rates that lead to

129 For example, there is large literature on how much of a tax should be imposed on petroleum to account for its implicit costs. See, e.g., Westin, *The Case For a Crude Oil Price Stabilization Tax,* 40 Env. Law Reporter 10328 (2010) for numerous references.

130 Cite Kaldor and Hicks here are the early proponents.

131 Professor Uwe Reinhardt discusses this anomaly incisively at Economix, When Value Judgments Masquerade as Science, August 27, 2010, http://economix.blogs.nytimes.com/2010/08/27/when-value-judgments-masquerade-as-science/?_r=0.

132 See Westin, When One-Eyed Accountants Are Kings: A Primer on Microeconomics, Income Taxes, and the Shibboleth of Efficiency, 69 Minn. L. Rev. 1099 (1985).

excessive tax planning.

Resources wasted in adjusting to transitions in the tax laws The principal objection is that a legislative fiscal change—including an increase or decrease in tax rates -- itself will force wasteful adaptation to the tax in the transition to the tax and thereafter. For example, having heard of the proposed tax increase that starts next year, the well-heeled taxpayer may accelerate his income to avoid having it fall into next year and may defer his deductions, even though all this may be to the detriment of his overall business planning.

Tax laws that unintentionally distort behavior compared to a tax-neutral situation. Here, dead-weight losses are forfeited utilities as a result of a legislative change. A common example involves tax-exempt fringe benefits in employment that not all employees assign full value to. For example, after the tax change, R may deploy his capital into investments that offer tax shelter in the form of depreciation deductions on property R borrowed to buy. If enough people do this, the price of real estate will rise solely because of the tax.

Even benign distortions can lead to deadweight losses. For example, when some "compensation" or economic benefits provided to employees can be excluded from gross income, but cash wages cannot be excluded, the difference in tax treatment can change the preferences of individuals as to the kind of compensation they seek. The result may be that workers get a form of tax-free benefit when they really would rather have cash or some other taxable benefit if it were not for the difference in tax treatment. The tax exemption for employer-provided means under IRC § 119 is an example. If the employer's costs for the two forms (cash paid to employees or meals furnished to employees) are the same and if both are deductible (or not) by the employer, the employees may be worse off than if they could have chosen among various benefits all of which were taxable or all of which were tax-free. Indeed, they may be worse off by more than just the amount of revenue collected by the government or the amount of revenue lost by the government in granting the tax exclusion.

> **Example:** Suppose an employer can offer either a $100 per month pay raise in cash or $100 (cost to the employer) of a tax-exempt meals on the premises. One employee might be indifferent between the two in a world with no income tax, or prefer the cash somewhat, and yet be influenced to choose the free meals costing $100, even if they are only worth $80 to the employee, if there is a 30% income tax in effect. (After a 30% tax, the $100 of cash wages yield only $70 to the employees, whereas the $80 worth of meals aren't taxed and yield an $80 after-tax benefit; it is only the after-tax return that the employee compares in making her choice.) An employee whose union chooses the meals over the cash

> does not like the food offered, but who has no individual choice in the matter, will be badly affected. She would have preferred the cash and the choice of using the cash for other purposes. Assuming she thinks the meals are worth only $75 (even though costing the employer $100) she will probably choose the meals rather than the $70 of after-tax cash. So the employer is spending $100 but the employee is getting only $75 in value, a $25 "deadweight loss" to the economy. The result is sub-optimal, since it causes a misallocation of resources in the economy in the form of excessive production and consumption of meals on the premises, compared to what the allocation would have been in the absence of this element of the tax law. [133]

Unduly complicated tax laws. Economists overlook this issue. A good example is IRC § 263A, an inexcusable provision that imposes monumentally complicated rules to force capitalization of a long list of items, replete with exceptions and limitations, all in order to make a up a revenue loss from other aspects of the Tax Reform Act of 1986. To many it is a lawyers' and accountants' relief act.

High tax rates and excessive tax planning. Another set of questionable claims runs as follows. High tax rates induce taxpayers to engage in the sterile activity of tax planning and employ small armies of tax specialists who dedicate their labor to tax avoidance. [134] That is true, but it is also true that lately legal reforms, including promptly-issued regulation, have largely shut down such activities[135] and that experts are subjected to disclosure requirements[136] and possible penalties[137] that make their more nefarious work too risky to undertake. It seems clear that it is the recent enactment of the passive loss rules[138] and IRS regulation of practice before the IRS[139] along with some prominent criminal prosecutions[140] that shut down the tax shelter industry, not the gentle persuasion of slightly lower rates. This objection boils down to a form of "inefficiency" which is discussed below in connection with macroeconomics. In addition, some

---

133 A less technical way to think of the subject is that the revenue leakage that resulted from allowing the meals exclusion was poorly managed in that it added unjustifiably little to the national welfare.

134 See Martin Feldstein, Tax Avoidance and the Deadweight Loss of the Income Tax, 81 Rev. Econ. & Stat. 674, 679 (1999) (demonstration and implications of avoidance as deadweight loss);Doernberg, A Workable Flat Rate Consumption Tax, 70 Iowa L. Rev. 425 (1985).

135 *See, e.g.*, Martha Neil, IRS Tightens Tax Shelter Rules, 4 No. 2 ABA J. E-Report 5 (2005); Governmental Attempts to Stem the Rising Tide of Corporate Tax Shelters, 117 Harv. L. Rev. 2249 (2004).

136 See, e.g., 31 CFR § 10.35(e)(1) (disclosure of certain compensation arrangements).

137 See, e.g., IRC §§ 6700 and 6701.

138 IRC § 469.

139 See Circular 230, embodied in 31 C.F. R § 10.3.

140 See J. Scott, *Tax Shelters: Risky Business,* Forbes Magazine Nov. 8, 2013 (criminal convictions and large penalties extracted from lawyers and law firms).

planning is socially useful, such as making larger charitable contributions because of their reduced after-tax cost.[141]

A haunting consideration is that as long as tax planning costs less than tax savings, shrewd taxpayers will pay for the planning, which suggests that rates should be flattened. Conversely, the argument that only high rates invite planning would seem suspect. If human greed is infinite, as microeconomics generally presumes, then any tax that can be neutralized for less than the cost of doing so will fall under attack.

The primary competing tax proposals

There are periodic calls for a consumption tax[142], including a progressive one,[143] but no matter what the exact design or its wisdom, it has the serious practical political disadvantage of exempting income from investments and exacting a disproportionate share of revenues from low-income workers who spent virtually all that they earn on necessities.[144] It is a proposal that never goes away and appears regularly as a Congressional tax policy consideration.[145] The other common proposal is for lower rates and a broader and more coherent tax base.[146]

The Decline of Content and the Rise of Lobbyists and Financed Ideology

Today's Sophistry goes vastly beyond anything seen in the seemingly naïve days of Classical Greece. It is mechanized. Congress is bedeviled by a ground force of well-paid

141 See Peter Diamond, Optimal Tax Treatment of Private Contributions for Public Goods with and Without Warm Glow Preferences, 90 J. Pub. Econ. 897, 901-03 (2006).

142 Similarly, there are proposals for a national value added tax, a topic with a large literature. There are important benefits, including the opportunity to improve exports by virtue of a manufacturer's ability to receive rebates of the tax and to impose such taxes on incoming goods. One author claims a broad VAT set at about 12.5% on the entire population plus an exemption from income taxation for people earning under $100,000 per year could be a substitute for the income tax for the bulk of the population. M. Graetz, *100 Million Unnecessary Returns: A Fresh Start for the U.S. Tax System*, 112 Yale L.J. 261, 282 (2002) (arguing for a tax system that combines a 25% income tax on incomes over $100,000 plus a VAT). An enormous amount of ink has been spilled on this topic and there is no need to spill further ink here. Once again, it is a materialistic consideration.

143 See, M. Graetz, *Implementing a Progressive Consumption Tax*, 92 Harv. L. Rev. 1575, 1601 (1979)

144 See, e.g., J. Repetti, *Democracy and Opportunity: A New Paradigm in Tax Equity*, 61 Vand. L. Rev. 1129 (2008) (lack of national consensus on best tax system and lack of consensus on goals of government; case for progressive income tax with few deductions as preferable to consumption tax).

145 See, e.g., *Present Law and Background Relating to the Tax Treatment of Retirement Savings* (April 13, 2012 JCX-32-12).

146 See *See* Jane G. Gravelle, *Practical Tax Reform For a More Efficient Income Tax,* 30 Va. Tax Rev. 389 (Fall 2010).

lobbyists numbering over 10,000[147]representing a vast array of special interest groups, and each is hired for its ability to deliver Congressional help and votes. Honest open debate is not on their minds, and with good economic reason; their success at overcoming popular demands can be legendary, as in the case of the power of the NRA to prevent any serious effort at gun control.

There is also an air force of well-financed ideologues, drumming their messages to shape public opinion. Policymakers and politicians are not the only targets of their propagandizing; the media and the public itself are also in their sights. These organized interest groups generally direct their political message to the citizenry,[148] largely on the theory that such targeting not only sways the public but also in turn attracts the attention and fear of members of Congress.[149] The most sinister practical effect is that it limits the discretion of the politicians which, in turn, affects the direction of public policy.[150] This indirect form of lobbying can be effective for ideologically minded groups, even including exempt organizations[151] and churches.[152]

Another concern is how ideological interest groups spend money on political action committees (PACs) to influence elections and how citizens view and vote for candidates.

---

147 Lobbyists are required to file a registration for each client on whose behalf a contact is made is a certain dollar threshold is met. See William P. Browne, Groups, Interests, and U.S. Public Policy, 84-85 (1998). This means one lobbyist suffers multiple filings with the Clerk of the Senate, such that the total number of filings cannot accurately reflect the number of lobbyists. The Center for Responsive Politics used data from the Senate Office of Public Records, however, to calculate 11,344 individual registered lobbyists who have actually lobbied in 2013. Reuters reported that there was a record of 15,137 registered lobbyists in Washington in 2007, also relying on data from the Center for Responsive Politics. United States Government Accountability Office, Lobbying Disclosure/Observations on Lobbyists' Compliance with Disclosure Requirements GAO-09-487 p. 5, (2009).The Washington Post also uses similar figures, but again they are based off of data from the Center for Responsive Politics. Lobbying Database, available at http://www.opensecrets.org/lobby/ The Post blames the decline in the number of lobbyists on a change to the lobbying rule made in 2007. Id. Robert Repetto, states that "the number of registered lobbyists in Washington grew from approximately 10,000 to 25,000" between the years 1996-2005. Robert Repetto, The Need for Better Internal Oversight of Corporate Lobbying, 50 Challenge, no.1 pg. 76 (2007). Repetto, however, provides no source or citation for his numbers.

148 Id. at 85.

149 Id. One aspect of this coercion is the "scoring" of politicians to identify cases where their votes do not hew the ideological line they claim they will follow. An example appears in Steven M. Graves and Christopher Peterson, , *Usury Law and the Christian Right: Faith-Based Political Power and the Geography of American Payday Loan Regulation,* 57 Cath. U. L. R. 637, 685 (2008) concerning Christian organizations scoring politicians with respect to the issue of usury and payday loans.

150 Id. at 86.

151 David M. Anderson, Political Silence at Church: The Empty Threat of Removing Tax-Exempt Status for Insubstantial Attempts to Influence Legislation; 2006 BYU L. Rev. 115, at 115-6 (2006); see also Chase Manderino, Understanding the Lobbying Efforts of a Church: How Far Is Too Far; 2009 BYU L. Rev. 1049, at 1049-50 (2009).

152 Manderino at 1050.

The concern is over groups spending money to elect particular candidates.[153] McKay conducted a study to determine what types of interest groups spend more money on electing certain candidates, or advancing certain ideological goals, instead of traditional lobbying expenses.[154] Analysis of the results of this study "shows that more ideologically extreme groups do seem to favor PAC contributions over lobbying expenditures."[155] McKay draws from this study the conclusion that the main purpose of campaign contributions among ideology-driven groups (at least, those in the sample), appears to be to help certain candidates win office, rather than to secure access to or influence politicians after the elections.[156] This is consistent with interest groups striving to advance ideological goals.

While there are many groups that present secondary issues, such as tax-exempt organizations; as a whole, ideological-based interest groups are free to advertise their cause to the public through mass media or "propaganda." Aside from the rules governing the use of PACs, there do not appear to any rules governing the use of such forensic efforts, nor is there any distinction in the rules regarding lobbying between ideological interest groups and more traditional lobbying groups. While the marketing of a group's message to the general public may be extremely similar in nature to propaganda, scholars appear to have little interest in the distinction. The following three headings illustrate the kind of word craft that is pitched to the public as part of the privately paid propaganda campaign.

Class warfare versus fairness and "ability to pay"

The words "class warfare" conjure up imagery of massive labor unrest and terrifying Stalinist purges and simply ignores the great discourses of Classical Greece and the patient labors of the Utilitarians. Thrasymachus the Sophist would be proud of this invention.

Conversely, the demand for "fairness" resonates intuitively and is popular with liberal politicians, but provides no framework for defining fairness or calibrating it, and as a result seems like a desperate last resort. The Tax Legislative Committee Reports are devoid of references to Utilitarian theories of taxation[157] and the Congressional Record

---

153 Amy McKay, "The Effects of Interest Groups' Ideology on Their PAC and Lobbying Expenditures," Business and Politics: Vol. 12: Issue 2, Article 4 pg. 1 (2010) Available at: http://www.bepress.com/bap/vol12/iss2/art4.

154 Id. at 1-3.

155 Id. at 9.

156 Id.

157 Performed Westlaw search of Federal Taxation Legislative History database using search term "Utilitarian." Performed on December 1, 2013. Resulted in one hit which was not relevant and which re: H.R. 4333 and the utilitarian value of artists' work.

has no apt references.[158] On the other hand, "ability to pay" rears its head everywhere in both the Congressional Record[159] and Committee Reports.[160] The problem is that the term lacks a foundation; it could be a clumsy reference to Utilitarian theory or even to some moral precept, but to those who do not care for taxes, it also sounds just as much like a weak rationalization for the expropriation of private property, which makes it an easy target for its opponents and a poor surrogate for thoughtful Utilitarianism.

Income taxes as destroyers of capital and employment

The arguments about taxing the wealthy can be worthy of Vaudeville comedy. It is a regular claim that reduction in top tax rates will profoundly stimulate investments in productive undertakings.[161] However, when legislative proposals suggest that taxes should be raised on the top strata the immediate objection is that increasing taxes on the rich will result in only modest revenue increases. It is heard whenever such increases are proposed, [162]but when proposals to cut tax rates are in the wind, lobbyists insist that the rich will save a great deal of money, which they will invest in productive activities.[163] Both statements cannot be true, but in the realm of sophistry over fiscal issues it does not matter.

The surprising dissonance between popular preferences and current income tax rates

Although one might think the present structure of income tax rates sits well with the public, a recent study suggests that the American citizenry would flock to a Swedish model of how to distribute wealth and are unaware of how extreme the distribution of

---

158 Westlaw search of Federal Taxation Congressional Record database on December 1, 2013, using search term "Utilitarian." It generated 35 hits, none of which were relevant.

159 Id. 329 hits about 33% apt.

160 Performed Westlaw search of Federal Taxation Legislative History database using search terms "ability to pay." The search was performed on December 1, 2013, and generated 80 hits, 30 of which appeared to be relevant, basing relevance on hits that discussed a taxpayer's ability to pay a tax (regardless of whether "ability to pay" was a factor in the tax or not; if a taxpayer's ability to pay a tax was mentioned, I treated it as relevant.)

162 See, e.g., John Stossel: Tax The Rich? The Rich Don't Have Enough. Really. (tax –based expropriations from billionaire as insufficient source of revenue). Available at thttp://www.forbes.com/sites/danbigman/2012/04/03/john-stossel-tax-the-rich-the-rich-dont-have-enough-really/.

163 See, e.g., Want Economic Prosperity for Everyone? Cut the top tax rates, not the bottom. http://www.redstate.com/cmndr45/2012/07/10/want-economic-prosperity-for-all-cut-the-top-tax-rates-not-the-bottom/

wealth in America really is.[164] The authors performed a nationally representative online poll the upshot of which was that (1) the participants greatly underestimated the degree of the disparity of wealth in America (not very surprising), and (2) by constructing an ideal distribution that was far more equitable than their erroneously low estimates of the true distribution. Above all, there was a remarkable level of agreement. Even Republicans preferred a more equal distribution of wealth than the status quo, although they also preferred to maintain some disparity. The authors could only speculate as to why poorer people did not press for greater equality:

> "First, our results demonstrate that Americans appear to drastically underestimate the current level of wealth inequality, suggesting they may simply be unaware of the gap. Second, just as people have erroneous beliefs about the actual level of wealth inequality, they may also hold overly optimistic beliefs about opportunities for social mobility in the United States . . . , beliefs which in turn may drive support for unequal distributions of wealth. Third, despite the fact that conservatives and liberals in our sample agree that the current level of inequality is far from ideal, public disagreements about the causes of that inequality may drown out this consensus . . . Finally, and more broadly, Americans exhibit a general disconnect between their attitudes toward economic inequality and their self-interest and public policy preferences . . . , suggesting that even given increased awareness of the gap between ideal and actual wealth distributions, Americans may remain unlikely to advocate for policies that would narrow this gap. "[165]

The participants were subject to the so-called "Rawls constraint" for determining a just society namely ' that they were required to imagine that if they joined this country, they would be randomly assigned to a place in the distribution such that they could wind up anywhere in that distribution. This powerful philosophical construct is the product of John Rawls as part of his study of distributive justice laid out in *A Theory of Justice*, in

---

164 Michael I. Norton and Dan Ariely, Building a Better America—One Wealth Quintile at a Time, 6 Perspectives on Psychological Science 9 (2011). The former author is with the Harvard Business School and the latter is with the Psychology Department at Duke University.. Some estimates suggesting that the top 1% of Americans hold nearly 50% of the wealth, topping even the levels seen just before the Great Depression in the 1920s." p. 9.

165 Id. at p. 12 (citing Benabou, R., & Ok, E.A., Social Mobility and the Demand for Redistribution: The POUM Hypothesis. 116 Quarterly Journal of Economics, 447-487 (2001); Charles, K.K., & Hurst, E., The Correlations of Wealth Across Generations, 111 Journal of Political Economy, 1155-1182, (2003); Keister, L.A., Getting Rich: America's New Rich and How They Got That Way (2005); Alesina, A., & Angeletos, G.M., Fairness and Redistribution, 95 American Economic Review 960-980 (2005); Piketty, T., Social Mobility and Redistributive Politics, 110 Quarterly Journal of Economics 551-584 (1995); Bartels, L.M., Homer Gets a Tax Cut: Inequality and Public Policy in the American Mind, 3 Perspectives on Politics 15-31 (2005); Fong, C., Social Preferences, Self-Interest, and the Demand for Redistribution, 82 Journal of Public Economics 225-246, (2001)).

which this influential American philosopher advances a model of justice derived from a hypothetical situation in which the parties assume they do not know whether they are rich or poor, intelligent or simple and so forth (commonly referred to as operating behind a "veil of ignorance"). Rawls proposes that parties would hypothetically choose commonly acceptable principles of justice, including as to matters of the distribution of wealth. Importantly, he asserts that the participants would all prefer to assure that the prospects of the least prosperous were accommodated. His ideas have influenced the thinking of serious modern economists.[166] The outcomes of the experimentations by Norton and Arieley square neatly with Rawls' propositions, and despite the actual outcome of highly skewed distribution of income and wealth and historically low taxes on income, there is strong reason to believe the US public favors greater progressivity of tax rates.

Interestingly, animal studies show that monkeys have a strong sense of fairness and in the opinion of a leading author that sense is likely innate and a function of evolution, and is impliedly significant for humans.[167] Another aside is theological; in the New Testament at Mark 12:41-44 Jesus observes that the poor widow who gave her last coin (a mite) gave more than all the rest, insinuating the compatibility of utility theory and Christianity. It is possible that this Christian thread is subconsciously woven into the fabric of modern progressive taxation.[168]

CONCLUSION

The trajectory of progressive taxation is discomforting, at least if one selects the period from early Greece to early Twenty-First Century America. We begin with principled thinking about how to form a comfortable society living with moral scruples during Classical Greece to the Enlightenment's (or at least Jeremy Bentham's) sincere mathematical inquiry into how to adjust relationships within society in order to maximize collective enjoyment to something more demoralizing than mere Sophistry.

166 See Anthony Atkinson & Joseph E. Stiglitz, Lectures on Public Economics (McGraw Hill 1980) pp. 339- 340 comparing social welfare functions of Bethamitie objectives versus Rawlseian objectives. A perusal of the subject index at the back makes it clear that Bentham and Rawls remain of great importance in fashioning economic policies. Stieglitz won the Nobel Memorial Prize in Economic Sciences in 2001.

167 Sarah F. Brosnan, Nonhuman Species' Reactions to Inequity and their Implications for Fairness, Social Justice Research, Vol. 19, No. 2, June 2006 (Ó 2006) DOI: 10.1007/s11211-006-0002-z. This is part of rich literature. See footnotes at end of Brosnan's article.

168 This is a growing literature exploring the relationship of taxation to religion See especially, Susan P. Hammill, An Argument for Tax Reform Based on Judeo-Christian Etics, 54 Ala. L. Rewv. 1 (2002) and (Ajay K. Mehrotra, "Render Unto Caesar . . .": Religion/Ethics, Expertise, and the Historical Underpinnings of the Modern American Tax System, 40 Loy. U. Chi. L.J. 321, (2009) (insights include that later 19th and early 20th Century populist pressure for progressivity in taxation was subordinated in public dialogue to economists theories in belief that the latters' justifications for progressivity were the more compelling in public debate).

The obvious problem is that while the concept of fairness is a stubborn one and may even be a part of human evolution, it reduces to little more than a word and a sensation when opposed to the pseudo-science of economics and the unthinking collective urge to maximize Gross Domestic Product. Unless and until the concept of fairness is given a more formal character, it is likely to remain too elusive to inject itself into public debate with the force it is entitled to.

The stakes are high. Societies with vastly disparate distributions of wealth and power breed cynicism and have the potential to become unstable or at least dysfunctional.[169] while failure to tax adequately exacerbates the problem by unfairly casting the burden of public debt onto younger generations. [1] Nobel Prize winner, economist Joseph E. Stiglitz put it this way in The Price of Inequality: "inequality may be at once cause and consequence of a breakdown in social cohesion over the past four decades."[170] He clarified his proposition with this chilling observation:

> "The more divided a society becomes in terms of wealth, the more reluctant the wealthy are to spend money on common needs because they can simply purchase such things as security, clean environment, etc. I would add that the poor are also less likely to cooperate with the wealthy in highly unequal societies. Which is how inequality contributes to the breakdown of the fragile cooperative equilibrium."[171]

Aristotle would surely agree.

Adding these concerns to the usual dry list of policy considerations that normally apply to shaping tax laws would be a healthy improvement, and the job of getting it included would be a worthy task for tax scholars and policymakers. A robust public debate would also surely help, but the political context makes it unlikely. It is surely an understatement to say that what Madison saw as the indispensable ingredient of civic virtue is lost in Washington, D.C. and it is disturbing.

---

[170] Joseph E. Stiglitz, The Price of Inequality, How Today's Divided Society Endangers our Future xi, p. 62 (2012). Stiglitz is a Nobel Prize winner and, among other achievements, was appointed Chairman of the Council of Economic Advisers in 1995.

[171] Id. at p. 93.

Drinking Smoke[1]

Don Stacy, M.D. dABR[2]
Joshua Nguyen[3]
Walter E. Block, Ph.D.[4]

I. Introduction

The United States are experiencing one of the biggest social movements in their history. Mirroring the era of alcohol prohibition, cannabis is slowly undergoing a process of decriminalization and gradual acceptance in society. The first States to legalize the recreational use of cannabis were Colorado and Washington, with many more attempting to follow their example. These two governments have a year to decide whether cannabis will be regulated by the State or be assimilated into the private market. Petitions have been sprouting across the country, in States like Missouri, Montana, Oregon, and Nebraska, for decriminalization and legalization of cannabis.[5] The movement is forcing the federal government to evaluate the situation meticulously.

In section II of this paper we discuss the demand for marijuana. Section III is given over to a discussion of an analogous case, the prohibition of alcohol. In section IV we argue in favor of the legalization of marijuana. The burden of section V is to discuss cracks in marijuana prohibition: the fact that this law seems to be on the way out. We conclude in section VI.

II. Demand for Marijuana

---

[1] The authors thank Jordan Reel for helpful comments on an earlier draft of this article. The usual caveats always apply.

[2] Independent Scholar, 13317 Westbury Way, Goshen, KY 40026, tel: (606) 369-4246, http://donstacy.com, anarchist1972@yahoo.com

[3] Research Assistant, Loyola University New Orleans, 6363 St. Charles Avenue , New Orleans, LA 70118, jknguye2@loyno.edu

[4] Harold E. Wirth Eminent Scholar Endowed Chair and Professor of Economics, Joseph A. Butt, S.J. College of Business, Loyola University New Orleans, 6363 St. Charles Avenue, Box 15, Miller Hall 318, New Orleans, LA 70118, tel: (504) 864-7934, fax: (504) 864-7970, wblock@loyno.edu

[5] Altieri, Erik. "8 States May Legalize Marijuana This Year – Did Yours Make the List?" *NORML Blog Marijuana Law Reform 8 States May Legalize Marijuana This Year Did Yours Make the List Comments.* NORML, 09 Feb. 2012. Web. 08 Apr. 2013. <http://blog.norml.org/2012/02/09/8-states-may-legalize-marijuana-this-year-did-yours-make-the-list/>.

The demand for cannabis has become more apparent with its ubiquitous appearance in movies such as *Pineapple Express*, *Ted*, *A Very Harold and Kumar 3D Christmas*, *This is the End*, and *Your Highness*.

Pew Research, an American think tank organization based in Washington D.C., performed a nationwide survey on people's views on marijuana in March of 2013. The results were released in April of 2013 and revealed that 52% of Americans support legalization of marijuana while 45% oppose it. This is the very first time a majority of Americans surveyed have supported marijuana legalization. The research showed that, in all demographics, support for marijuana has increased. The morality of smoking marijuana has even become a non-issue, for half of Americans now say it is not a moral issue.[6] The most important statistics may be the following: "More than half of young people (56%) say they have tried marijuana, and 27% say they have tried it in the past year… About half of those 30- to 49 [in age] (51%) and 50-64 [in age] (54%) have tried marijuana."[7] The high prevalence of use[8] assists by pushing legalization of marijuana even faster. However, seeking legalization at the state level may be more successful than at the national level.

The Substance Abuse and Mental Health Services Administration (SAMHSA) publicly released the *Results from the 2012 National Survey on Drug Use and Health: Summary of National Findings* on September 3, 2013.[9] The findings and associated tables illuminate the results of an annual survey, the National Survey of Drug Use and Health (NSDUH), of 70,000 Americans 12 years of age or older. Though the survey is a State operation, which should always be contemplated with skepticism, the NSDUH is currently and widely viewed as the most comprehensive study of drug and alcohol use in the United States. The relevant marijuana data are as follows:

1. 7.3% of Americans surveyed in 2012 confirmed marijuana use in the past month; this is an increase from 7% in 2011 and 6.2% in 2002 (this difference was statistically significant at the 0.01 level)
2. 12.1% of Americans surveyed in 2012 confirmed marijuana use in the past year; this is an increase from 11.5% in 2011 (this difference was statistically significant at the 0.05 level) and 11% in 2002 (this difference was statistically significant at the 0.01 level)

---

6 Ibid.

7 Ibid.

8 And its normalization.

9 Substance Abuse and Mental Health Services Administration, Results from the 2012 National Survey on Drug Use and Health: Summary of National Findings, NSDUH Series H-46, HHS Publication No. (SMA) 13-4795. Rockville, MD: Substance Abuse and Mental Health Services Administration, 2013.

3. 42.8% of Americans surveyed in 2012 confirmed marijuana use in their lifetime; this is an increase from 41.9% in 2011 and 40.4% in 2002 (this difference was statistically significant at the 0.01 level).

Thus, the American State's own data reveals that the use of marijuana has steadily expanded over the past decade.

III. Prohibition of Alcohol

During the 1920's, alcohol demand was also high, if not more so. Despite the 18th Amendment,[10] the demand for alcohol was large enough that people were willing to risk the danger to traffic alcohol across borders. This paved the way for gangsters and other entrepreneurs to capitalize on supplying alcohol to dry counties. In a similar fashion, the demand for cannabis has provided a large incentive for people to supply marijuana regardless of the law. The many prohibition-related issues are a clear sign that law enforcement does not work the way government intends. The most basic law of economics, supply and demand, illustrates the fact that anyone can get what he wants if he is willing to pay the price. "Authorities" should not fool themselves into thinking they have complete control over people's lives. Regulations on the market process are only a nuisance and hold back economic prosperity. Higher federal officials are, however, professionals at dispersing cost and concentrating wealth.

Men seek to accomplish their goals whether it hurts or benefits the many. When a person obtains a position of power, it is easy to be swayed by luxurious gifts and donations. As a new law or policy is being debated, it is important to inquire who shall benefit. Behind every veil there is a hidden truth. During the 1920's prohibition, companies like Coca-Cola and Walgreens profited. Today, police unions, pharmaceuticals, breweries, and prisons are capitalizing on the illegality of cannabis.[11]

Interest groups are intimately involved in the drafting of much legislation. These groups have the most to gain from lobbying for various laws. The benefits from the legislation they endorse are often at the expense of society. Prohibition is no exception. Coca-Cola was one of the most successful companies to cash in on the prohibition of alcohol.

[10] The 18th Amendment established prohibition of alcoholic beverages in the United States, which made the production, transport, and sale of alcohol illegal, but not consumption.

[11] Fang, Lee. "Exclusive: Why Can't You Smoke Pot? Because Lobbyists Are Getting Rich Off of the War on Drugs." *Republic Report.* 7 Mar. 2012. Web. 29 Apr. 2013. <http://www.republicreport.org/2012/exclusive-why-cant-you-smoke-pot-because-lobbyists-are-getting-rich-off-of-the-war-on-drugs/>.

Coca-Cola was originally sweetened with wine, but after prohibition, John Pemberton[12] replaced the wine with sugar and sold it as an ideal temperance drink.[13] This allowed Coca-Cola to act as a replacement for alcoholic beverages as well as a mixer for the harsh alcohol being illegally imported.

Alcohol prohibition was considered by many an attempt to improve American society. Despite these intentions, "[p]rohibition failed to eliminate alcohol, and even exacerbated many of the social ills related to its consumption, because government is limited both by its knowledge of how people react to regulation and also by the incentives faced by the regulators themselves."[14] Overall, prohibition was a complete failure. Alcohol could not be forcibly removed from the American lifestyle. However, this law was enacted through a democratic process, which presumably represented the will of the majority of people; but this was simply not the case. The most powerful lobbyist for prohibition, the Anti-Saloon League (ASL), artificially decreased the Congressional representation of those against prohibition by manipulating the Congressional district lines. All of those against prohibition were grouped into a few districts, while those in favor of prohibition occupied many districts. The abuse of district lines was dubbed gerrymandering, named after Governor Elbridge Gerry of Massachusetts. Gerrymandering created an overrepresentation of those for prohibition in the State legislatures as well as in Congress.[15] Anti-prohibition groups could not check the ASL as it slowly increased its influence on legislation. The ASL, legally, took advantage of the system with the help of various other interest groups. This event is a prime example of State folly and the ability of different private groups to work together for a common but unjust end.

Without such support, the ASL could not have implemented prohibition nor kept it on the books for as long as it did. Interest groups, like the ASL, were and still are the backbone for the persistence of prohibition. Companies like Coca-Cola and Walgreens recognized and capitalized upon the profit potential from prohibition. Coca-Cola tripled its sales due to lack of competition and Walgreens expanded from 20 to 525 drug stores.[16] Even the American Medical Association (AMA) realized the profit potential. The AMA initially supported the concept of prohibition, claiming that alcohol had no

---

[10] Doctor John Pemberton was a pharmacist from Atlanta, Georgia who invented Coca-Cola in a three-legged brass kettle in his backyard.

[11] Solar Navigator "History Coca Cola John Pemberton." Coca Cola Marketing History. Solar Navigator, Web. 03 Apr. 2013.

[12] Rogers, Douglas. "The Fiasco of Prohibition." *The Freeman : Foundation for Economic Education.* FEE, 22 Dec. 2010. Web. 03 Apr. 2013. <http://www.fee.org/the_freeman/detail/the-fiasco-of-prohibition>.

[13] Ibid.

[16] Ibid.

value. After passage of the Volstead Act,[17] however, the AMA asserted that alcohol could be used to treat 27 different conditions and ailments.[18] Thus, alcohol prohibition was initially promoted under the slogan of improving everyday life; but behind the veil, one finds interest groups pulling all the strings in the legislation process. Unfortunately, citizens today are still being deceived by the same tactics used almost a century ago.

IV. Prohibition of Marijuana

Cannabis prohibition was first introduced in the U.S. by the State of California in 1913. However, it was an obscure amendment promulgated by the State Board of Pharmacy. The issue received no attention from the press and was part of the earliest anti-narcotics campaign inspired by anti-Chinese sentiments in California.[19]

The prohibition of marijuana by the State of Utah is an interesting story. Mormons in Utah were unable to practice polygamy after the practice was outlawed in 1910. This led many Mormons to move out of the country in order to maintain their polygamous lifestyle. Many relocated to Mexico and experimented with marijuana. When they decided to return to Utah, some brought marijuana with them. The head of the Mormon Church did not tolerate this development and influenced the legislature to outlaw marijuana in 1914.

The Rocky Mountain and southwestern States, consisting of Texas, New Mexico, Colorado, and Montana, banned marijuana due to racial prejudice towards Mexican.[20] The white population was wary about a large immigration of Mexicans seeking better economic opportunities. Marijuana accompanied the immigrants.

---

[15] The Volstead Act was enacted in 1919 to provide enforcement for the Eighteenth Amendment, prohibiting the manufacture and sale of alcoholic beverages. President Woodrow Wilson vetoed the act, but it became law after Congress voted to override the veto.

[16] Rogers, Douglas. "The Fiasco of Prohibition." *The Freeman : Foundation for Economic Education*. FEE, 22 Dec. 2010. Web. 03 Apr. 2013. <http://www.fee.org/the_freeman/detail/the-fiasco-of-prohibition>.

[17] Gieringer, Dale H. "The Origins of California's 1913 Cannabis Law." *CA NORML Costs of Prohibition*. May 2012. Web. 03 Mar. 2013. <http://canorml.org/background/ca1913.html>.

[18] Olsen, Carl. "The Early State Marijuana Laws." *Schaffer Library of Drug Policy*. Web. 03 Apr. 2013. <http://www.druglibrary.org/olsen/dpf/whitebread05.html>; The racism towards Mexicans was so high that a Texas legislator openly said, "All Mexicans are crazy, and this stuff (marijuana) is what makes them crazy." Montana's law said, "Give one of these Mexican beet field workers a couple of puffs on a marijuana cigarette, and he thinks he is in the bullring at Barcelona."

After witnessing such bans, northeastern States outlawed marijuana as well, fearing that users of other drugs like heroin or cocaine may switch to marijuana.[21] This view is the opposite of the debunked gateway theory espoused by many drug warriors today.[22]

The initial criminalization of marijuana was never based on any actual studies. It was the ignorance of foreigner-fearing States, which led to negative views of cannabis. Before the bans, cannabis was being used as medicine, and today it is used legally in some States. At this point, many wonder why marijuana remains outlawed. The answer is the power of interest groups. Today, there are five big interest groups lobbying against the legalization of marijuana: police unions, private prison corporations, alcohol and beer companies, pharmaceutical corporations, and prison guard unions.[23] Each group has a vested interest in the continued criminalization of marijuana. Despite the formation of many organizations for the legalization of cannabis such as NORML,[24] they have little power compared to those lobbying to continue prohibition. The police and prison guard unions and the private prison corporations fear the loss of federal grants, while the alcohol and pharmaceutical companies want to avoid additional competition. The interest groups understand very well that State power is a perfect opportunity to concentrate benefits and disperse costs. Robert Taylor, a journalist for PolicyMic, says, "Contrary to public school folklore, more often than not the state protects wealthy and established interests at the expense of consumers and the little guy, wrapping it in the rhetoric of the public good."[25]

The public good is at most a secondary or tertiary concern to interest groups when lobbying for government legislation. Police unions, for example, obtain multi-million dollar federal grants for eradicating marijuana on the street. These provide incentives for interest groups to oppose legalization via a chain effect phenomenon: the more cannabis "criminals" thrown in prison, the more federal money transferred from the State to prison owners and guards.[26] A notorious example of interest groups fighting for prohibition involves a Californian named John Lovell. He built an entire business based

[21] Ibid.
[22] Joy, Janet et al, Editors. "Marijuana and Medicine: Assessing the Science Base." National Academies Press. 1999. Retrieved 2013-09-18.
[23] Fang, Lee. "The Top Five Special Interest Groups Lobbying To Keep Marijuana Illegal." *The Top Five Special Interest Groups Lobbying To Keep Marijuana Illegal Comments.* Republic Report, 20 Apr. 2012. Web. 03 Apr. 2013. <http://www.republicreport.org/2012/marijuana-lobby-illegal/>.
[22] National Organization for the Reform of Marijuana Laws.
[25] Taylor, Robert. "Marijuana Legalization Being Crushed By Special Interest Groups." PolicyMic. Apr. 2012. Web. 29 Apr. 2013. <http://www.policymic.com/articles/7835/marijuana-legalization-being-crushed-by-special-interest-groups>.
[26] Fang, Lee. "Exclusive: Why Can't You Smoke Pot? Because Lobbyists Are Getting Rich Off of the War on Drugs." *Republic Report.* 7 Mar. 2012. Web. 29 Apr. 2013. <http://www.republicreport.org/2012/exclusive-why-cant-you-smoke-pot-because-lobbyists-are-getting-rich-off-of-the-war-on-drugs/>.

on marijuana prohibition. He was paid handsomely by various policing groups to stop the passage of Proposition 19[27] in California. Police unions, prisons, and guards all contributed to pay Lovell for his services. This is a practice all too common in the United States.

The fundamental nature of the State did not change at the start of the 21st century. The only differences are the companies and interest groups lobbying the State and what legislation they desire. Today pharmaceutical companies favor marijuana and hemp prohibition in fear that legal cannabis would replace the majority of the drugs available at the local drug store. The most unfortunate groups that back marijuana prohibition are alcoholic breweries and distilleries. They understand the damage prohibition can produce socially and economically better than any other industries, yet they still lobby for it. From a self-interest standpoint, the prudent choice is for many businesses to support prohibition because legal marijuana has the potential of drawing customers away. With large government intrusions on what can be sold as goods, people are unable to freely trade with relatively low transaction costs. Instead, government provides a medium for companies like alcohol and pharmaceuticals to restrict alternatives from entering legal trade through lobbying. The idea of free trade is skewed by government intervention.

Another argument in favor of legalization is that the government cannot possibly win the "War on Drugs." For, every time the State "wins" a battle, they strengthen, not weaken, the "enemy." With that sort of result, it should occasion no surprise that the overall prospects for success from the point of view of the State are slim to none. How does this work? Suppose that the State interdicts a shipment of cocaine, and burns it.[28] What does this do to the price of this drug? It cannot be denied that with a shift of the supply curve to the left, ordinary supply and demand analysis indicates that the price will *rise*. But with a higher price, there are more profits to be made in this industry. And, as well known, a boost in revenues will call forth more suppliers, more product, more drugs. Namely, a *failure* of the drug prohibition occurs, which, presumably, has as its goal to lessen, not expand, the quantity available for general use. If a "war" cannot possibly be won, Catholic just war theory[29] suggests that it should not be undertaken in the first

[27] Prop 19 or the Regulate, Control & Tax Cannabis Act was a ballot initiative that would have legalized marijuana-related activities, allowed local governments to regulate such activities, permitted local governments to impose and collect marijuana-related fees and taxes, and authorized various criminal and civil penalties.

[28] In many cases, no burning takes place. Rather, the police seize these substances for themselves, since they are so valuable. But, arguendo, let us make the best case for the drug war, which abstracts from this sort of graft, and the undermining of law and order.

[29] McElroy, Wendy. 2011. "Can a Principled Libertarian Go to War?" July 6; https://mises.org/daily/5431/.

place,[30] or, if we find ourselves in the midst of one, we should exit from it as soon as possible.[31]

There is one argument in favor of drug legalization that we need not support: that with the end of prohibition, these substances will be commonly manufactured, sold, purchased and the government will tax them at every stage. While many commentators favor legalization on this ground, among others, we do not follow them there. Rather, we maintain that drugs should be decriminalized *in spite of* this undoubted correct prediction. We argue that the State, the source of this problem in the first place, already has far too much financial support with which to undermine freedom. The last thing it need is more funds with which to pursue its harmful practices.

V. Cracks in Marijuana Prohibition

This country has grown more tolerant and the majority of society no longer has such negative views toward ethnic groups. Government officials have grown more tolerant but the policies they promote often contradict what they actually believe. Despite marijuana being classified among the most harmful drugs with no usefulness, a federal judge in 1976 ruled that the FDA must provide marijuana for Robert Randall.[32] Randall suffered from glaucoma and no other drug could effectively combat the condition.[33] The contradiction between the ruling and the law at the time forced the government to compromise. A program was created that would provide each recipient with a half pound of marijuana in the form of 300 pre-rolled joints. However, the war on drugs escalated and the program stopped accepting members in 1992. Those who are members continue to receive their medicine. Supplying citizens with medicinal marijuana while claiming it has no health benefits is a mind-numbing contradiction. Government officials say that there is no contradiction because the program is no longer accepting new patients. This flawed logic has fortunately been minimally influential, for the majority of the States (27) have decriminalized cannabis or permit it for medical use.[34]

[30] Rothbard, Murray N. "Just War" in Denson, John V., ed. 1997. The Costs of War: America's Pyrrhic Victories. New Brunswick, N.J.: Transaction Publishers.

[31] Vance, Laurence M. 2008. Christianity and War and Other Essays Against the Warfare State Vance Publications; 2nd edition.

[32] Robert Randall became the first legal pot smoker in the United States since prohibition of marijuana. He also became the poster child for medical marijuana use around the country.

[33] Duara, Nigel. "4 Americans Get Pot from US Government." *Yahoo! News*. Yahoo!, 28 Sept. 2011. Web. 03 Apr. 2013. <http://news.yahoo.com/4-americans-pot-us-government-070245907.html>.

[34] On the other hand, at least two presidents (Clinton, Obama) had admitted to violating drug laws. If these were consistently applied, both would have been charged with crimes. The failure of government to obey its own laws was also witnessed during prohibition in the 1920's. The Michigan State Police "raided Detroit's Deutches Haus and found 800 people inside, including a Michigan congressman, a sheriff, and Detroit Mayor John Smith," all consuming alcohol (Teller). See also Cachanoski, 2013.

With the majority of the States already easing the laws against cannabis, it is obvious that social views of cannabis are changing. There are petitions to legalize marijuana in almost every State. Marijuana legalization is no longer something the State can ignore. More people are incarcerated for marijuana than for any other drug. This fact is evidence that people are not willing to simply stop using it because laws deem it harmful (despite the variety of medical studies showing that the cannabinoids in marijuana practically make it a miracle plant). For example, one of marijuana's most prominent uses is for pain relief. A primary fear of drug companies is that marijuana might replace the pain relievers available at many retailers.

VI. Conclusion

Prohibition is a messy business that has never been proven effective. The aftermath sometimes is more terrifying than the times before prohibition. The drug war on cannabis is as illogical as wearing shoes on your head. The studies presented to government officials that show cannabis is anything but harmful have been dismissed or ignored. One of the most prominent examples of such an event involved President Richard Nixon asking the National Commission on Marijuana and Drug Abuse to compile a study on the effects of marijuana. The Commission reported the following: "Neither the marijuana user nor the drug itself can be said to constitute a danger to public safety. Therefore, the Commission recommends ... [the] possession of marijuana for personal use no longer be an offense, [and that the] casual distribution of small amounts of marijuana for no remuneration, or insignificant remuneration no longer be an offense."[35] Nixon and Congress chose to ignore the commission's conclusion. Nixon went as far as pressuring the chair of the Commission to reject its findings.[36] The logic of continuing cannabis prohibition is as faulty as the reasons the laws were drafted in the first place. Simply put, the laws against cannabis and the chronic propaganda against cannabis are due to rational ignorance.

References

Altieri, Erik. "8 States May Legalize Marijuana This Year – Did Yours Make the List?" *NORML Blog Marijuana Law Reform 8 States May Legalize Marijuana This Year Did Yours Make the List Comments.* NORML, 09 Feb. 2012. Web. 08 Apr. 2013.

[35] "Nixon Commission Report Advising Decriminalization of Marijuana Celebrates 30th Anniversary." *NORML: Working to Reform Marijuana Laws.* NORML, 21 Mar. 2002. Web. 8 Apr. 2013. <http://norml.org/news/2002/03/21/nixon-commission-report-advising-decriminalization-of-marijuana-celebrates-30th-anniversary>.

[36] Ibid.

<http://blog.norml.org/2012/02/09/8-states-may-legalize-marijuana-this-year-did-yours-make-the-list/>.

Cachanoski, Ivan, Vannia J. Zelaya and Walter E. Block. 2013. "Drug legalization: Rescuing Central America from the claws of crime." *The Journal Jurisprudence*, Vol. 21, March, pp. 9-25; http://www.jurisprudence.com.au/juris21/Cachanosky.pdf; http://www.jurisprudence.com.au/back.htm.

Duara, Nigel. "4 Americans Get Pot from US Government." *Yahoo! News*. Yahoo!, 28 Sept. 2011. Web. 03 Apr. 2013. <http://news.yahoo.com/4-americans-pot-us-government-070245907.html>.

Fang, Lee. "Exclusive: Why Can't You Smoke Pot? Because Lobbyists Are Getting Rich Off of the War on Drugs." *Republic Report*. 7 Mar. 2012. Web. 29 Apr. 2013. <http://www.republicreport.org/2012/exclusive-why-cant-you-smoke-pot-because-lobbyists-are-getting-rich-off-of-the-war-on-drugs/>.

Fang, Lee. "The Top Five Special Interest Groups Lobbying To Keep Marijuana Illegal." *The Top Five Special Interest Groups Lobbying To Keep Marijuana Illegal Comments*. Republic Report, 20 Apr. 2012. Web. 03 Apr. 2013. <http://www.republicreport.org/2012/marijuana-lobby-illegal/>.

"Gerrymandering." Encyclopedia Britannica. Encyclopedia Britannica Online. Encyclopedia Britannica Inc., 2013. Web. 08 Apr. 2013. <http://www.britannica.com/EBchecked/topic/231865/gerrymandering>.

Gieringer, Dale H. "The Origins of California's 1913 Cannabis Law." *CA NORML Costs of Prohibition*. May 2012. Web. 03 Mar. 2013. <http://canorml.org/background/ca1913.html>.

Joy, Janet et al, Editors. "Marijuana and Medicine: Assessing the Science Base." National Academies Press. 1999. Retrieved 2013-09-18.

McElroy, Wendy. 2011. "Can a Principled Libertarian Go to War?" July 6; https://mises.org/daily/5431/.

"Nixon Commission Report Advising Decriminalization of Marijuana Celebrates 30th Anniversary." *NORML: Working to Reform Marijuana Laws*. NORML, 21 Mar. 2002. Web. 8 Apr. 2013. <http://norml.org/news/2002/03/21/nixon-commission-report-advising-decriminalization-of-marijuana-celebrates-30th-anniversary>.

Olsen, Carl. "The Early State Marijuana Laws." *Schaffer Library of Drug Policy*. Web. 03 Apr. 2013. <http://www.druglibrary.org/olsen/dpf/whitebread05.html>.

Pew Research. "Majority Now Supports Legalizing Marijuana." *Pew Research Center for the People and the Press*. 4 Apr. 2013. Web. 29 Apr. 2013. <http://www.people-press.org/2013/04/04/majority-now-supports-legalizing-marijuana/>.

Rogers, Douglas. "The Fiasco of Prohibition." *The Freeman: Foundation for Economic Education*. FEE, 22 Dec. 2010. Web. 03 Apr. 2013. <http://www.fee.org/the_freeman/detail/the-fiasco-of-prohibition>.

Rothbard, Murray N. "Just War" in Denson, John V., ed. 1997. The Costs of War: America's Pyrrhic Victories. New Brunswick, N.J.: Transaction Publishers.

Solar Navigator "History Coca Cola John Pemberton." Coca Cola Marketing History. Solar Navigator, Web. 03 Apr. 2013. <http://www.solarnavigator.net/sponsorship/coca_cola.htm>.

Substance Abuse and Mental Health Services Administration, *Results from the 2012 National Survey on Drug Use and Health: Summary of National Findings*, NSDUH Series H-46, HHS Publication No. (SMA) 13-4795. Rockville, MD: Substance Abuse and Mental Health Services Administration, 2013.

Taylor, Robert. "Marijuana Legalization Being Crushed By Special Interest Groups." *PolicyMic.* Apr. 2012. Web. 29 Apr. 2013. <http://www.policymic.com/articles/7835/marijuana-legalization-being-crushed-by-special-interest-groups>.

Teller. "The Windsor-Detroit Funnel: Prohibition in Detroit." *Walter P. Reuther Library.* 17 Jan. 2012. Web. 03 Apr. 2013. <https://www.reuther.wayne.edu/node/8334>.

Vance, Laurence M. 2008. *Christianity and War and Other Essays Against the Warfare State* Vance Publications; 2nd edition.

Method and Metaphysics:

A Legal Historian's Canon

C.G. Bateman*

Abstract

In the following research I discuss a number of issues which are fundamental to my understanding of how best to reconstruct past human events from the methodological outlook of a legal historian. Herein one will find an explanation *of* and justification *for* the various aspects of the historical method and philosophy I employ in my larger research area involving the Roman Emperor Constantine, the Christian Church, and state sovereignty. I also discuss some lines of intersection between modern day legal actors and historians to show how their common goal of getting to the truth of a question may encourage the former to consider using some of the same hermeneutical tools as the latter. History as a discipline has always been primarily concerned with humans and their actions, and this has been noted by many historians: Marc Bloch and R.G. Collingwood come to mind as being two of the strongest proponents of this dictum.[1] Since the field of human events in the past is so large, I suggest it behooves us, then, not to confine ourselves too narrowly within our investigations concerning the hermeneutical tools we employ in the study of the multivariate ways that humans have acted and existed since their appearance some two-hundred thousand years ago: and to this end I employ *Sub specie aeternitatis* as my research's inclusive-contextual *raison d'être*. This perspective requires an acknowledgment that scholarly observations about the reality of the human condition from other disciplines must be employed in the effort to be as wide-ranging in our research method gathering as the *historical* method will allow: and thus a number of key contributions from authors in various academic fields will be discussed to highlight the relative importance of their ideas to my own. I will be using examples within my own

*The author wishes to thank Professors Dennis Pavlich and John B. Toews for their helpful comments on the paper as it was being put together. I also wish to thank Ron Balden for his many introductions to scholars who have found their way into my 'historian's canon' over the years.

[1] Marc Bloch, *The Historian's Craft*, trans. Peter Putnam (Hong Kong: Manchester University Press, 1954; 1991): 22-27. Bloch wrote the *Historian's Craft* in 1944 during World War II while in prison for his activities as a member of the French Resistance. He was tortured and shot to death by the Nazi Gestapo in June of 1944. His tragic death prevented him from finishing this essay. R.G. Collingwood, *The Idea of History* (Oxford, Clarendon Press: Oxford, 1946, 1949). Collingwood wrote "What kinds of things does history find out? I answer, *res gestae*: actions of human beings that have been done in the past." (9).

area of study[2] to engage these ideas and this will better acquaint the reader with how I approach historical data. This discussion will be purposely focused on the foundational ideas upon which my own historical method is based. This will enable the reader to better appreciate how it is that I as a historian come up with suggestions about what it was in history that most likely happened. I conclude that as a historian my highest goal must be to offer an imaginative re-construction of an historical event and its concomitant personages which is based on extant data, but which also must engage in a participatory re-thinking pursuant to the motivations of the characters involved such that the end result can be read as an intelligible whole.

Introduction

The Future is dark, the present burdensome; only the past, dead and finished, bears contemplation. Those who look upon it have survived it: they are its product and its victors. No wonder, therefore, that [they] concern themselves with history.

S.R. Elton, *The Practice of History*†

The symbolic universe also orders history. It locates all collective events in a cohesive unity that includes past, present, and future.

Peter L. Berger and Thomas Luckmann, *The Social Construction of Reality*††

...the history of everything amounts to the thing itself.

John Lukacs, *Historical Consciousness*†††

All of us are a product of the past, and in this one observation lay much of the historical method itself. This notion lays in the foundational idea that there always remains

† G.R. Elton, The Practice of History (New York: Thomas Y. Crowell; Sydney University Press, 1967), 1.
†† Peter L. Berger and Thomas Luckmann, *The Social Construction of Reality: A Treatise in the Sociology of Knowledge* (Garden City, N.Y. : Doubleday, 1966), 95.
††† John Lukacs, *Historical Consciousness: The Remembered Past* (New Brunswick (U.S.A.): Transaction Publishers, 1968; 1985;1994; 2003), ix.
[2] My research is concerned with the history of the theory and practice of sovereign power in the Western World, specifically focusing on the marriage of Church and State under Constantine in the early fourth century CE, and the nascent transfer of powers that took place at that time.

continuity with the past no matter how significant a break a historical event may seem to be in the eyes of future generations. It seems the idea "we cannot escape our own past" is true for history itself: *everything* is connected, however tangentially at the edges. Even in light of this, the historian is also aware of how little of human history we actually have any idea about. Historians' approach their discipline with an irony that may not be sidestepped: life for humans is on average only around eighty to one hundred years on the outside, and we only appeared on the scene as "history-makers" one hundred thousand years ago, on the inside.[3] In truth, there is a universal history before ours which stretches some thirteen billion years. Our lives are not merely brief by comparison: in fact, given an eighty year average, we occupy less than a thousand millionth of a percent given that stretch of time – and, in fact, even our possible earthly existence hinged on a process of the formation of the Universe itself which introduced the planet Earth only two-thirds of the way along. If we were more strict and only measured from our own time backwards, using the earliest extant written records dating from the fourth millennium B.C.E as our starting point for comparison, then we are still talking about six thousand years, and then our lives jump to an unimpressive .013% represented against the lesser whole.[4] As Carl G. Gustavson – whose observations inspired my own – pointed out over fifty years ago: if and when we study, as many do, *institutions* from the past, then "[t]he human being, with his puny life span, is but a pygmy walking among giants whose growth and decline must be measured in terms of centuries."[5] Looking at the relationship, for instance, between Constantine the Great's Roman Empire and the Christian Church is to make suggestions about two *major* institutions that existed a mere seventeen centuries ago. All this speaks to our perspective of looking behind us in the human story and it must be conceded that historians will never have the big picture of human life on earth if for no other reason than we only have written records for six of the last hundred thousand years. On the other hand, Marc Bloch has noted that the student of the present is in scarcely better standing, since almost everything we learn in life is from others and very little, by comparison, is acquired from our own senses.[6] Whether one studies the past or the present we learn almost everything we know from others. We are physically dependent by definition, and epistemologically dependent to well-nigh the same degree. So what we do know about human history is limited, and it comes to us almost entirely from others.

---

[3] The estimates range from 80,000 to 250,000 years.

[4] M.C. D'Arcy, *The Meaning and Matter of History: A Christian View* (New York: Noonday Press – Farrar, Straus and Giroux, 1959), 18: "History is a late growth in the evolution of man."

[5] Carl G. Gustavson, *A Preface to History* (New York: McGraw-Hill Book Company, Inc., 1955), 4.

[6] Bloch, *Historian's Craft*, 50. Bloch writes: "Because the individual, narrowly restricted by his senses and power of concentration, never perceives more than a tiny patch of the vast tapestry of events… and because, moreover, he possesses an immediate awareness of only his own mental state, all knowledge of mankind, to whatever time it applies, will always derive a large part of its evidence from others. In this respect, the student of the present is scarcely any better off than the historian of the past."

Even in light of the foregoing, it is still true from our perspective that the Juggernaut wheels of historical interpretation – based on the human species' legacy of extant records – not only roll forward but ostensibly crush all our previous 'complete histories' upon which the actions and lives of our predecessors were informed and structured, and upon which new total histories are being re-configured to fit the discoveries made during the costly march of human progress and enlightenment which strove and strives for equality for all people.[7] It is in this evolution of human existence throughout history that human events instantiate and then at times are recorded for us at the initiative and selection of 'historians' who choose to write such accounts, from as early as Herodotus onwards. This 'selection' of 'facts', though, presents a particular problem. As E.H. Carr writes, "[t]he belief in a hard core of historical facts existing objectively and independently of the interpretation of the historian is a preposterous fallacy…."[8] The fact is that what historians sometimes treat as facts are not facts at all but an imagined story based on the biases of an, let's say, ancient author who gave the historian their facts in the first place: and this has led to all sorts of maltreatment of human beings throughout their history.[9] The problem for historians ought to be clear at this point: if past histories upon which the normative worldviews of a given society were once based have been proven to be false on new evidence or jettisoned on the basis of the, often, consequentially monstrous treatment of other humans, and if new more evidentially based histories replace them and new worldviews of a more benign nature conquer the older worlds, then what will occur when what is new is old again? In other words, even though the leading edge of historical explanation in the 1200's is so far different from modern historical research as to belong to a different category, we have to acknowledge that if what soothed society then is enough to make us recoil in horror now, we ought then to write our history with a humility which forces us to produce work in the realm of suggestion, rather than authoritative explanation: or worse yet, proclamation. To begin with, then, the story of history is only partially known for a very small part of what is in truth, *actual* human

7 Every movement towards shared resources and human freedom and equality since the Protestant Reformation would suffice as evidence for this claim, although we could go further back even still. The Reformation, the Enlightenment, the French Revolutions, the British and American Revolutions, and the Abolition of Slavery are all important movements which exemplify the point raised.

8 E.H. Carr, *What is History* (Harmondsworth, Middlesex: Penguin, 1961; 1973), 12. He goes on: "I collected fifteen or twenty volumes on my shelves and took it for granted that there, recorded in these volumes, I had all the facts relating to my subject. Let us assume – it was very nearly true – that those volumes contained all the facts about it that were then known, or could be known. It never occurred to me to inquire by what accident or process of attrition that minute selection of facts, out of all the myriad facts that must once have been known to somebody, had survived to become *the* facts of history." (13).

9 *Vide infra.*

history. Truly, as the single most important ancient text in Western Culture puts it, "…our days on earth are but a shadow."[10]

Legal Actors and Historians

It is perhaps exactly because our time on earth is limited that systems of laws have arisen throughout history to insure that humans are able to enjoy and participate in as much of that lifetime as possible: and we punish those who deprive others of these rights in the varying degrees such participation is thwarted. When such rights to life and liberty are deprived, one person vis-à-vis another, legal actors are then engaged to insure appropriate laws are enforced. The most prominent of these actors, perhaps, is the one with the final decision-making power, the judge. Every judge is a historian of sorts. They deal with adjudicating past events. While in a Common Law context it is true they are considering evidence from only two parties' arguments, they are still trying to determine who is responsible for the various aspects of an event involving persons. In this way, just like historians of all stripes, the judges, by definition, are reacting to events that happened in the past: their role, then, much like the police, is largely reactive rather than preventative. In a dispute between two litigants, lawyers will provide the judge with evidence about "what happened." And yet there is the rub, judges are *provided with* evidence, whereas the historian *collects it* themselves. While this is a significant difference, oftentimes judges are dealing with enough of the available evidence to reconstruct an event to a satisfactory degree based on that same evidence. Their main task is to interpret how given events interact with persons based on the aforementioned laws. The responsible historian, also, will want as much of the available evidence as possible to insure that their reconstructions of past events and suggested motives of the actors are as grounded in what can reasonably be inferred from the evidence as possible, but rarely will they learn facts about an event in the detailed way a modern day judge would.

Even in light of this, historians, then, are very much judges of a sort: yet they are also called upon to wear the hats of lawyers, *amicus curiae*, and interveners pursuant to their own trial which seeks to uncover the truth about a past event. Their focal point, as with the judge, is a past event involving persons. Yet unlike the judge in a court of law, historians are not constrained by any laws except their method, which in most cases is anchored to the requirement that their judgements need to be reasonably connected and inferable pursuant to the evidence which they have at hand. In terms of the historical

[10] *Job* 8.9b, 14.1-2, *Holy Bible: New Revised Standard Version Containing the Old and New Testaments and the Deuterocanonical Books*. Bruce Metzger, ed., Second edition, (Peabody, Massachusetts: Hendrickson Bibles & Oxford University Press, 2007), 357.

actors, historians are not required to prove the motives of these figures beyond a reasonable doubt, as in a criminal trial: their standard is much more akin to the civil law standard on the "balance of probabilities," given the evidence.

In most cases, as it is in my own research, historians are dealing with human stories wherein most if not all of the relevant characters to an event have long passed away. And with them in time goes most of the evidence concerning those peoples' lives: and yet if their contemporaries thought they were important enough figures, political or religious, etc., posterity has to varying degrees left us evidence of those real people who lived in 'actual history.'

With my own more general subject of Constantine and his Council of Nicaea, there is fortunately enough written by a variety of historical personages to give some of the more broad strokes about his life and activities, but nothing like a day to day journal. It is in this place of restricted amounts of evidence that the historian 'lives and moves and has their being,'[11] to quote a turn of phrase used by the Apostle Paul in a lecture given to philosophers in the Areopagus at Athens in the mid first century. Even here with Paul we find someone who was at that very moment engaged in a kind of historical reconstruction of events and was arguing as a lawyer would to convince, not one judge or even a panel of judges, but a rather large group of philosophers, that the new religion he was teaching people was based on solid evidence: now, in some sense, this group of philosophers was 'trying' him on the persuasiveness of the evidence he presented in his argument. Some of the 'judges' rejected his argument, others adjourned the hearing for another day to hear more evidence, and some were convinced on the evidence presented.[12] Those of us familiar with the machinations of appeal courts in common law jurisdictions today will be very familiar with these kinds of reactions coming from panels of judges ranging from arbitration boards to the Supreme Court. The law allows for judges to decide differently based on their interpretation of the written law, and with historians this same kind of flexibility exists as well: although it is acknowledged here that historians, most often due to the paucity of evidence, argue about what actually happened whereas modern day judges often know very well what happened but can disagree about how an event ought to be interpreted in light of the rubric of the laws upon which their decision must rest. Yet historians have to pay attention to laws as well, but these latter go by another name, method.

In this paper I will argue that for historians, our laws, our constitution if you will, is essentially the method which we self-impose on our researches that will give us the best chance of convincing our peers and various readers that our reconstructions of past

---

[11] *Bible*, NRSV, *Acts* 17.28, *New Testament*, 105. He is recorded as saying: For 'In him we live and move and have our being'; as even some of your own poets have said, 'For we too are his offspring.'
[12] Ibid., Acts 17.32-17.34, 105.

events and the motives of the people involved are reasonable and therefore acceptable, based on the evidence.

Getting to Method

For many centuries in our common past, history was not written by historian's per se, but rather by, as the old saying goes, the "victors," and those victors had a particular outlook, just as it is true of all historians.[13] One the other hand, history over the last one-hundred years or so has been and continues to be written most commonly by historians who adhere in general to the basics of the historical method such as being aware of continuity, change, relativistic outlooks, *inter alia*,[14] but such was not the case with Herodotus, Eusebius, or Augustine, for instance. These historians, it is true, wrote their histories based on what they had learned from witnesses and second hand evidence in oral or written form, in much the same way as we do today, but what colored their reconstructions of the past was their commitment to their particular world view which interpreted events in history as being part and parcel of their beliefs in the supernatural: for Herodotus, it was a recognition of the Greek pantheon of gods, and for the latter two the religion of Christianity. Josephus might be mentioned here as well, but he seems to this author to be less directed by personal and cultural bias and more attentive to the notion of a simple recording of events as best as he could reconstruct them.[15] For more recent historians the essential problem has remained the same, the indubitable fact that political views, methodological commitments, or a number of such biases are part of any written history, and the great quest for historians is to manage the biases of past historians and to keep their own biases out of their reconstructions as far as possible.

Such a difficulty intrinsic to history was highlighted in the latter part of the Renaissance by humanist skeptics such as Cornelius Agrippa (1486-1535) and Francesco Patrizzi (a.k.a. Franciscus Patricius, 1526-1597) who claimed the vices of historians included, for

[13] Carr points to two important truths about historians and their histories, "...you cannot fully understand or appreciate the work of the historian unless you have first grasped the standpoint from which he himself approached it; secondly, that that standpoint is itself rooted in a social and historical background. ...The historian, before he begins to write history, is the product of history." (39-40).
[14] *Vide infra.*
[15] Josephus was a former Jewish army commander who traded sides on being captured by the Romans. He wrote his historical accounts as an advisor and translator for the Emperor Vespasian and he was close friends with the Emperor's son Titus who led the siege on Jerusalem in 70 A.D. I have read all the historians mentioned herein and Josephus reads as being less concerned with religion and politics than the three others, and more of a pure chronicler. But as with any historian, we know that some of his bias would have made it in, but my point is that such bias is significantly less obvious than with the other three historians aforementioned.

Agrippa: first, being negligent and credulous in gathering data; second, they retail hearsay as truth; third, that some have observed but only see by halves; and that, fourth, for some they did not work with public records but their own conjectures; in short, most historians were seen by this skeptic as liars.[16] Agrippa writes:

> For historians are at such variance among Themselves, delivering several Tales of one and the same Story, that it is impossible but that most of them must be the greatest lyers in the World. For to omit the beginnings of the World, the Universal Deluge, the building of Rome, or of any other great city, from whence they generally commence the first beginnings of their Huge Narratives – of which they are altogether ignorant, of the other generally very incredulous, and of the third very uncertain what to determine. For these things being the most remote in time, more easily gain Pardon for Vulgar Error. But as to what concerns later times and ages, within the memory of our Ancestors, there is no excuse that can be admitted for their Lying.[17]

For Patrizzi's part, he added a theoretical dimension to this critque,[18] and noted that, first, if a historian were not present for the reported events, their veracity is not worth discussing because they rely on the unknown entity of the truthfulness of the accounts they cite; second, that even the observer will either be neutral or partisan and that with the latter we should expect distortion while the neutral party is not likely to have intimate knowledge of the situation; third, and further, that even if certain historians agree about a point it does not inhere that the truth is then established because they all may be relying on a shared rumor.[19] Patrizzi's contribution, according to scholar Julian H. Franklin, is that he postulated a "good historian," in the neutral observer, only to show that this person does not have the vital information.[20] Patrizzi claims that the pragmatic norm of history being the insistence that an observer have an "inside" story meets the pragmatic theory of politics which has the observer keeping the secrets to themselves, and thus an accurate and instructive narrative are shown to be incompatible goals.[21] Franklin comments: "[i]t is this incompatibility, finally, which underlies Patrizzi's "consolation." The human story, he concedes, is "truthful," but only *grosso modo* – in its coarser outlines – which means that it is "uninstructive."[22] As to their general effect on history and method, he writes:

[16] Julian H. Franklin, *Jean Bodin and the Sixteenth-Century Revolution in the Methodology of Law and History* (New York: Columbia University Press, 1963), 90.

[17] Henry Cornelius Agrippa, *The Vanity of Arts and Sciences* (London and Westminster, 1676), 27, as in Franklin, *Bodin and Revolution in Methodology in Law and History*, 95.

[18] Franklin, *Bodin and Revolution in Methodology in Law and History*, 96.

[19] Ibid., 96-99. Franklin is citing Francesco Patrizzi, *De historia dialogi X*, in *Artis historicae penus*, I.

[20] Ibid., 99.

[21] Ibid., 99-100.

[22] Ibid., 100. Franklin is citing Francesco Patrizzi, *De historia dialogi X*, in *Artis historicae penus,* I, 458-459.

> These attacks upon belief in history are a new achievement in the history of skepticism which is not surpassed until the nineteenth century. But they are of even greater moment for the theory of history, as an initial, if exaggerated, statement of certain fundamental principles of criticism. The most important, surely, is that all historians are subject to an element of doubt, that it cannot be presumed, in other words, that their statements are "exactly true." In the vices mentioned by Agrippa we have a primitive listing of the forms of historical distortion. And Patrizzi's finding that the plans and motives of an action are the class of subjects on which truthfulness is least to be presumed is not only ingenious but substantially correct. …The limitation of the skeptics, on the other hand, is their illegitimate demand for certainty, by which doubt is turned into an absolute.[23]

The exaggerations of these sixteenth century skeptics include, first, the fallacy that error proven in an author means complete mendacity; second, that from the untruthfulness of some we must assume the same of all, and worst of all, third, the inference that because history is inexact that it therefore must be useless.[24] And yet even though precursors, perhaps, to the excesses of post-modern philosophy in terms of epistemology, Franklin is correct in highlighting the fact that the observations of these skeptics pursuant to written histories were to become foundational ideas that were not again emphasized until the nineteenth century German revolution in the historical method which apparently brought us a, then, "new" approach to historical data.

One can see a very similar parallel existing between the assertions of the foregoing skeptics and a related problem highlighted by the twentieth century historian E.H. Carr: this historian observes that our knowledge, for instance, of Greece in the fifth century B.C. is defective primarily because it is a picture formed by a very small group of people in Athens, and barren of the perspectives of Spartans, Persians, the Athenian slaves, and a large number of other relevant groups.[25] We come back, then, to the fact that historians are susceptible to their own political views, methodological commitments, and/or a number of other such biases. Thus, when choosing one's important or significant facts, as the historian may do as influenced by the motives aforementioned, Carr explains that "…the standard of historical significance is [the historian's] ability to fit them into his pattern of rational explanation and interpretation."[26] On the idea of historical significance, historian John Lukacs separates the idea of an 'important' fact/event from a 'significant' one. He writes:

---

[23]Ibid., 101-102.

[24] Ibid., 102.

[25] Carr, *What is History*, 13. In another place he writes, "In the first place, the facts of history never come to us 'pure', since they do not and cannot exist in a pure form ; they are always refracted through the mind of the recorder." (22).

[26] Carr, *What is History?*, 105.

> For historical importance and historical significance are not the same things: while the opening of the transisthmian canal or the first automobile assembly line in 1914 are important rather than significant events, Mussolini's turn from international socialism toward a nationalist ideology, or the sudden jump in the American divorce rate – "minor" events, these – are significant rather than important.[27]

For Lukacs the latter examples are significant because they mark the emergence of tendencies which eventually became important, the example of Mussolini needing no elaboration.[28] So historians choose facts/events to suit their own research, it is true: but again, as Carr pointed out, the facts we are getting from history are from select individuals and can be coloured by a range of attitudes, aims, and convictions pursuant to the authors themselves. Thus, as Geoffrey Barraclough writes:

> It is still far too little appreciated that the history we read, though based on facts, is, strictly speaking, not factual at all, but a series of accepted judgements; and it is these generalized judgements, precisely because they are so plausible and so easily assimilated, that form the minds and colour the outlook of those who cannot know the fragility of the framework upon which they rest.[29]

It has been noted by more recent historians Martha Howell and Walter Prevenier that "any reality [facts] that lay behind the sources is, finally, inaccessible to us, no matter how skilled we are – and that we have to settle for studying the reality that sources construct rather than "reality" itself."[30] The only difficulty with this claim is that, first, no historian would claim to have uncovered the whole reality based on the sources, because the only way that could be true is if the historian lived through and witnessed the event, which is almost never the case with historical studies. Second, historians would not publish anything if they thought they could not reconstruct a picture which reflected part of the reality that likely was: in other words, even though *the* reality is lost, what that reality looked like in some respects can in many cases be sufficiently suggested, and *is* on an ongoing basis by most historians. In this respect I agree with G.R. Elton's astonishment at any claim purporting that nothing can be known about the past:[31] a great deal is known about the past, and we learn more about it every time more evidence comes to light which gives us more information about the events we happen to be concerned with.

---

27 Lukacs, *Historical Consciousness*, 130.

28 Ibid.

29 Geoffrey Barraclough, *History in a Changing World* (Oxford: Basil Blackwell, 1955), 14. Also quoted in part by Carr, *What is History*, 14.

30 Martha Howell and Walter Prevenier, *From Reliable Sources: An Introduction to Historical Methods* (Ithaca, NY: Cornell University Press), 149. See generally 148-150.

31 *Vide infra.*

Like Barraclough, John Lukacs eschews the idea of "facts." He wrote "I have come to dislike the word "Fact"... I have come to prefer the euphonious word "event" to "fact" whenever I can."[32] Lukacs justifies this by noting that "fact" is a somewhat dry, definite, and static word whereas "event" suggests life, flow, and movement,[33] and on this point I absolutely agree. Without question, then, the historian faces this double reality of the Aegis of Zeus which deflects the arrows of "historical facts" in the former's selection and interpretation of events, and on the other hand a Labyrinth in the style of Daedalus pursuant to the multivariate paths on which he may take the reader – and, by definition, themselves – based on his choice of facts. I venture to suggest that the risk to historians of finding themselves trapped like the Minotaur in a maze of selective facts and interpretation is then something to be wary of and prevented as far as possible by the admission of one's world view and an explanation to the reader of how one intends to keep it at bay: again, at least to the degree which may be reasonably expected by a critically minded reader.

C. Behan McCullagh suggests that although the bias of the historian is a real concern, it can be accounted for in three general observations.[34] The first point is that historians are seldom constructing their depictions of the past based directly on their personal values but rather to solve a problem or construct a hypothesis with relevant information.[35] Historians are trained to look at all the data relevant to their problem which is available,[36] and here I suggest this partly forces them not to move too far out of the bounds which have been set by what is generally agreed on as 'known' events of the past. Secondly, "...as historians gain a more precise knowledge of the conditions under which their descriptions of the past are justified, so they may become better able to assess their rational justification."[37] McCullah also notes that since a critic may be as biased as the historian he criticizes, only the hostile expert critic or an impartial critic are in a position to assess a historical description as warranted by the evidence, thus justified.[38] Thirdly is the simple fact that even close attention to standards of justification by the historian may not prevent a prevalent form of bias, that of not considering alternative explanations due to their own preconceptions.[39] In light of these observations, I suggest that due to the existence of, in most cases, expert and impartial critics in most of the major fields of history, that historians are then obliged not to wander too far afield in their re-constructions of the past, and if per chance they do, the idea that any widely published

---

32 Lukacs, *Historical Consciousness*, 103.
33 Ibid.
34 C. Behan McCullagh, *Justifying Historical Descriptions* (Cambridge: Cambridge University Press, 1984), 233-236.
35 Ibid., 233.
36 Ibid.
37 Ibid.
38 Ibid., 234.
39 Ibid.

work on a subject would escape the eyes of other historians of the same field is practicably impossible.

Further, and continuing from above, without question, we are forced to acknowledge that it is precisely because humans in the past took the time to record their own reconstructions of events that later generations of historians could even conceive of interpreting the events and motivations involved pursuant to the historical personages and institutions which may be at issue.[40] So while bias may be a concern, it is far from being an insurmountable obstacle to the wide consensus amongst historians on events that, due to the historians of antiquity and other written or physical evidence, have so many different sources of evidence that we consider them as close to a fact as one can get in historical study. Collingwood wrote, "[h]istory proceeds by the interpretation of evidence: where evidence is a collective name for things which singly are called documents."[41] On the other hand, those various evidences, such as writings, inscriptions, coins, and items not intended to inform the future about the life and times of the creator, have become invaluable tools for the historian. The physical evidence, referred to as "relics," are very helpful since, as with the *steles* (stela) that have been discovered, they not only contain information about people and places according to their inscriptions, they can also tell us the geographical location in which such objects were created and erected – and this can be determined in some cases by a building or monolith that clearly has not moved over the centuries, or by determining where the rock that was used to build the stele came from, or by other external and or written evidence that corroborates its current position, or by a combination of one or more these and other evidences. As with my own area of study, though, examining the actions of Constantine and the Christian Church and their revolutionary synthesis in the fourth century, we are left with almost exclusively documentary evidence pursuant to the events that led to this confluence of societal powers. Once this trajectory had been established by Constantine, though, we see much in the way of physical evidence throughout what was then the Roman Empire in edifices such as the City of Constantinople and the many Churches built at the Empire's expense. As Michael Lipka pointed out, what had been the international religion of Christianity and associated with diversity, in both their geographical locations and theological doctrines, was turned into a state religion of Rome where particular spaces and places were made more important by the vaulting not only of buildings,[42] but of a state enforced hierarchy of bishops who ostensibly signed off on

---

[40] While it is true that without written records, the role of the historian would not have developed as it did, and history would be the subject matter alone of the anthropologist and the archeologist. As it happened, though, historians now must account for "tracks" wherever they find them, and not simply confine themselves to the assemblage and interpretation of documents. Block noted that the primary characteristic of historical observation is, as François Simiand put it, a knowledge of the tracks left by those in the past. See Bloch, *Historian's Craft*, 54-55; See generally, 48-78.

[41] Collingwood, *Idea of History*, 9-10.

[42] Michael Lipka, *Roman Gods: A Conceptual Approach* (Leiden: Brill, 2009).

a single Christian doctrine of God, both of which began a long process of integration with the social and political frameworks of the Roman and Western European world.

Physical evidences such as the aforementioned can then be compared with the chronicled histories left to posterity since Herodotus, and we are then able to test the veracity of the latter's accounts and/or fill in details left out.[43] Now, in the case of Eusebius's monograph *Life of Constantine*, for instance, we are forced to acknowledge that it still remains the most important evidence historians have for Constantine even though it is written at many points in the style of hagiography. We also must, though, also take into account Bloch's observation: "…even those texts or archæological documents which seem the clearest and the most accommodating will speak only when they are properly questioned."[44] So too must any "history" be "questioned" with the use of other evidences. Collingwood wrote:

> [a historian] is reading the Theodosian Code, and has before him a certain edict of an emperor. Merely reading the words and being able to translate them does not amount to know their historical significance. In order to do that he must envisage the situation with which the emperor was trying to deal, and he must envisage it as that emperor envisaged it. …Thus he is re-enacting in his own mind the experience of the emperor; and only in so far as he does this has he any historical knowledge, as distinct from a merely philological knowledge, of the meaning of the edict.[45]

The general trajectory of these directives is that when writing on the subject of an historical event one must take account of not only the historical sources, but of both the immediate and extended contexts that give us our relevant variables for suggesting what the historical person was thinking and experiencing: thus helping us understand why they acted the way they did. We also are well advised to consult the relevant works of other historians, as well as all other relevant studies,[46] that came before us and have already engaged in this methodological process pursuant to the same historical people and events. Bloch's hope was that historians in future would tend to teamwork in their studies rather than relying on the Herculean efforts of one person:

But whatever the variety of accomplishments we may wish to ascribe to our best-equipped scholars, they will inevitably and, ordinarily very quickly, discover their own limitations. We have no other remedy than to substitute, in place of the multiple skills of a single man, the pooling of the techniques, practiced by different scholars, but all tending to throw light upon a specific subject. This method presupposes a spirit of

---

43 Marc Bloch, *Historian's Craft*, 60-63.
44 Ibid., 64.
45 Collingwood, *Idea of History*, 283.
46 Marc Bloch, *Historian's Craft*, 69.

teamwork. It also demands the preliminary definition by common consent of the several dominant problems. We are still all too distant from these goals. Nevertheless, in large measure, they will unquestionably govern the future of our science.[47]

While this trajectory has perhaps not always been adhered to in the environments of academic parsimoniousness and career padding,[48] it still remains a necessity for the serious historian and is easily detected in their work by a continual recognition of the relevant work of "others."

Metaphysics and History

> Philosophies of history, sciences of history, - all these there will continue to be: the fashions of them will change, as our habits of thought will change; each new philosopher will find his chief employment in showing that before him no one understood anything; but the drama of history is imperishable, and the lessons of it will be like what we learn from Homer or Shakespeare, - lessons for which we have no words.
>
> James Anthony Froude, *The Science of History*†

Is *actual* history truly beyond words? I suspect James Anthony Froude is right: historians, in their attempts to access history, are engaging in somewhat of a metaphysical exercise pursuant to their capacity to understand it, primarily because while imperishable in one sense, the events are, by definition, beyond the researcher's own experience. In this section I will discuss why I think this is and suggest what might be some resultant implications stemming from this idea.

It is *a priori* the case that historians' conclusions are dependent entities in so far as they are only the most recent link in causal chains going back to their sources: in other words, historians use the sources – including all relevant materials – at their disposal along with commentary on the sources which can be found on the linear time projection trajectory

---

47 Ibid.

48 Stanislav Andreski, *Social Sciences as Sorcery* (New York: St. Martin's Press, 1972), 187-197; 224-230.

† James Anthony Froude, *The Science of History*, Lecture: Royal Institution of London, February 5, 1864, as in *Modern Eloquence*, ed. Thomas B. Reed, vol. 4: Lectures F-M (Chicago: Geo. L. Shuman & Co., 1903), 467.

stemming from the earliest account of "their" event to the present.[49] Further to this and axiomatic for my own assumptions is the fact that human history consists of a concrescent[50] process wherein "everything is positively somewhere in actuality, and in potency everywhere,"[51] as Whitehead wrote concerning his ontological principle. In other words, the universe is a solidarity of many actual entities.[52] Actual or real history[53] is a living solidarity of this kind, and we know this because most of us accept the premise that we exist, and there is widespread consensus on the existence of our universe and, important here, for the actions of humans in the past which have led to our own existence in the here and *now*: except, in terms of time, as you read this, there goes the word 'now.' In truth, no sentence in its creation could ever exist wholly in the past or present: by definition and while in creation it is a combination of both. We are a people in motion, living on a planet in motion, within a galaxy in motion, and subject to the whims of a universe in motion. Even though we know these truths, illusions of stasis abound and have abounded throughout human history. The world was once thought to be still while the sun revolved around us, and when we examine a mountain, or a rock for that matter, it looks completely stable, and yet on the contrary it is in motion just like everything else on the planet. So too our experience of life can seem like it stops at times, and yet it moves at a tremendous rate even if we choose to remain motionless. Actual history is somewhat like the slow growth of a large tree which is actually constantly in motion and changing – contrary to any illusion of stasis[54] – and constantly

---

49 D'Arcy, *Meaning and Matter*, 16. I choose D'Arcy here for his concise wording: "Now from the beginning of recorded history men and women have been living on the evidence of others, and almost everything we think about and talk about is somewhere or other dependent upon the evidence of other people."

50 Alfred North Whitehead, *Process and Reality: An Essay in Cosmology*, *Alfred North Whitehead: An Anthology*, eds. F.S.C. Northrop and Mason W. Gross (New York: The MacMillan Company, 1953), 927: Whitehead's word "concrescence" is derived from the Latin verb for 'growing together.' The word conveys the notion of many things making up a complex and complete unity.

51 Whitehead, *Process and Reality*, 2.1, 608.

52 Ibid., 609.

53 When I refer to actual or real history I simply mean everything that has ever happened in the past, regardless of the fact humans were not there to witness it. It would be a very narrow minded perspective to think that only the appearance and spread of the species *Homo sapiens sapiens* should figure into the definition of the word 'history'. Historians such as Bloch attempt to separate "the history of historians" as the only history of interest to historians and surely this is correct in the main, and yet no one would deny the appellation "history" to subjects such as "history of the universe," "history of the cell," etc. Bloch emphasizes his own view in *Historian's Craft*, 22-27. G.R. Elton writes: "If [an] event were unknowable – if no evidence of it had survived at all – it would certainly be neither fact about the past nor historical fact – it would have ceased to ceased to exist and that piece of potential history would never have materialized – but it would still, of course, have occurred, independent of any historian." (56). Elton also used similar terminology to my own when he wrote: "… for ultimate history is what *actually* happened, even though we shall never be able to rediscover it in full or with total assurance." [Emphasis added] (56).

54 An interesting side in this discussion can be found D..M. Armstrong's response to Evan Fales in: Evan Fales, "Are Casual Laws Contingent?," *Ontology, Causality, and Mind: Essays in Honour of D.M. Armstrong*, eds. John Bacon, Keith Campbell, et al. (New York: Cambridge University Press, 1993):121-143. Armstrong writes: "Consider a stone today and that stone yesterday. Although, by hypothesis, it is 'the very same

converting the universe of which it is a part. Marc Bloch wrote "historical time is a concrete and living reality with an irreversible onward rush. It is the very plasma in which events are immersed, and the field within which they become intelligible."[55] G.R. Elton further points to the fact that unlike the natural sciences wherein experiments are "invented," and certainly manipulated, by the researcher, historians cannot invent their experiments and thus they are not able to "escape the first condition of [their] enterprise, which is that the matter he investigates has a dead reality independent of the enquiry."[56] In one sense, we might borrow from Aquinas's argument on God's existence from necessity, and rather than his penultimate premise 'something does exist now,' it becomes for historians, "something did exist then."[57] Human history, as only one part of

stone', this assertion of identity raises certain problems. In particular, the stone yesterday will have certain properties that the stone today lacks and vice versa. For instance, the temperatures of the stone at the two times may be incompatible with each other. But how is this possible if what we are dealing with is the identical subject of predication? ... There are various solutions on offer…. [but] the one we are interested in here, is to partition things that exist through time into two classes. Some things – genuine atoms and souls were the traditional examples – are in their nature completely unchanging; only their environment changes. As a result, a problem such as that of the incompatible temperatures cannot arise for these things. These things are strictly identical over time. Other things, such as stones, have only what Bishop Butler called a 'loose and popular' identity over time." (147). At another place in the same collection, Armstrong writes: "Armed with this distinction between absolute and relative sameness, we can make good sense of some things said by past philosophers, in particular Bishop Butler's "loose and popular identity (1736, Dissertation: 'Of Personal Identity') and Hume's 'fictitious' or 'feigned' identity (1738/1888, Book 1, Part IV, Section 2). …. Again, we say that a thing or person today is the very same thing or person that existed yesterday. This was the problem that Butler and Hume were discussing. Some metaphysicians hold that. In favourable cases at least (unchanging atoms; souls), this is a matter of absolute identity. Others maintain that all that is ever involved is a relative identity. On this second view absolute identity cannot be maintained over time. What we have instead is a class of short-lived objects (time slices) that (more or less) form an equivalence class. The nature of the equivalence relation is a matter of controversy here. Some favour spatiotemporal continuity, others some sort of causal connection between the short-lived objects. But without adjudicating that dispute here. I will just say that I take the relative identity view, thus showing that the cat can jump in different directions in different situations." D.M. Armstrong's response to David Lewis in: David Lewis, "Many, but Almost One," *Ontology, Causality, and Mind: Essays in Honour of D.M. Armstrong*, eds. John Bacon, Keith Campbell, et al. (New York: Cambridge University Press, 1993): 41.

55 Bloch, Historian's Craft, 27-28.

56 Elton, *Practice of History*, 53. On this same point, he also writes: "The historian cannot verify [like the natural scientist using the scientific method]; he can only discover and attempt to explain. In the work of discovery he has the assurance that he is looking for something that once had existence and is therefore, in theory, discoverable." (54). Also, "[t]he independent and real existence of historical events implies that, in theory at least, they can be observed absolutely, and for a very large number of somewhat basic facts this holds good." (59). While one may not agree with Elton's "observed absolutely" we can still take the nub of his point seriously. See related comments from Elton at 61ff.

57 Thomas Aquinas (1225-1274): this thirteenth century Roman Catholic philosopher's argument for God from necessity basically posits the following: 1. Beings are either dependent [like a baby on its mother] or independent; 2. If everything were an dependent being, then nothing would exist now [the implication being that the illimitable examples of dependent beings we have discovered so far in the universe (people, stars, galaxies, frogs, etc.) imply that if we go back far enough in the causal chain we will find that by definition a first being could not have been dependent because then they would not be correctly the first

a larger *actual* history of the universe, is also a story of concresence ('growing together') in which human kind is constantly caught in motions of growth and change in which the building blocks of our lives, atoms, are the exact same as those constituting the much larger and largely unknown universe. Collingwood wrote, "are not natural processes really historical processes, and is not the being of nature an historical being?"[58] He also challenges the implications of an evolutionary conception of nature worked out by the likes of Whitehead and other philosophers,[59] which resolve nature into history and he writes "…it might seem to be provided by Mr. Whitehead's doctrine that the very possession of its attributes by a natural thing takes time."[60] Collingwood counters by proposing that as history is not the same thing as 'change' *simplicter*, it is also not like 'timefulness,' meaning that just because a natural entity inhabits time does not give the former's actions the status of actions as we think of them pursuant to human history.[61] For Collingwood, an event has an outside, entailing bodies and their movements, and an inside, consisting in terms of thought. For him an action is the unity of these two aspects pursuant to an event.[62] In contrast to what I herein have identified as "actual history," including all events in the universe from the flowering of a yellow rose in sunlight to the creation of galaxies, Collingwood separates off the historian's idea of history as dealing with actions consisting of events with an outside and inside. He concludes that "…the processes of events which constitute the world of nature are altogether different in kind from the processes of thought which constitute the world of history."[63] Like most historians, Collingwood argues for a separation between the history of humans and the history of everything,[64] but we must always remember that the history of humans is within, dependent on, and subordinate to the history of everything.

If my suggestion of an "actual history" is beyond the historian's reach, it does not mean we are not subordinate to it, it only means that the historian's concerns are circumscribed by their incapacities as humans and, as with most living creatures, their insatiable appetite for pleasing themselves: and for humans, this entails "knowing" themselves, for which history is a potent and well used elixir. John Lukacs insists that the "history of everything amounts to the thing itself,"[65] which may come across at first blush as implying that, for instance, the history of the Nicene Creed is in fact that remote

being]; 3. Something does exist now; 4. Therefore an independent being must have existed as the progenitor of all we know – dependent beings.

58 Collingwood, *Idea of History*, 210.

59 Collingwood, *Idea of History*, 211: The author mentions three: Whitehead, M. Bergson, and Mr. Alexander.

60 Ibid., 212.

61 Ibid., 212.

62 Ibid., 213.

63 Ibid., 217.

64 Ibid., 215.

65 Lukacs, *Historical Consciousness*, ix.

event in 325 all by itself, as an event within actual history. This cannot be true, of course, because if that were the case we would have no access to its history whatsoever, and this is not what Lukacs meant. If I read him correctly, the history of the Nicene Creed would be its existence and all manifestations thereof from the moment it was first written until the present moment where someone in a church somewhere is invariably repeating a version of it as you read this. In this sense, then, we can separate in our minds the reality of an "actual history" versus the idea of a "history of," the latter being the dependent and yet constantly emerging reality within "actual history". With this in mind, then, the historian who examines event-entities occurring at one tiny point in time on such a massive trajectory of actual history must keep in mind the context for his or her own subjects of study,[66] and it is almost always the case that their suggestions about historical subjects can be contextualized adequately with deference to contemporary instantiational and situational grids of evidence.

Historians' claim an event as a subject of study but in almost all cases, he or she had nothing to do with the event itself, unless they study historical events that they experienced firsthand, and in that case we are dealing with a primary source, and one in which a single perspective is gained. If the alleged event only involved that one historian and no other person, their account would be the only information we had, but it would not ensure that the event actually happened, or that the description of the event accorded with what physically happened, hence it begins to tread already, just one abstraction away from the event itself, on the verge of the metaphysical. Related to this is the claim that predictability, and I would include objective observation, is intrinsically impossible in the study of a system of which the observer forms a part.[67] Even in light of this, G.R. Elton's rightly warns historians off taking this variable too far when he writes:

> But that men cannot ever eliminate themselves from the search for truth is nonsense, and pernicious nonsense at that, because it once again favours the purely relativist concept of history, the opinion that it is all simply in the historian's mind and becomes whatever he likes to make of it.[68]

Collingwood, perhaps, states it slightly more delicately:

66 Carr writes, "The men whose actions the historian studies were not isolated individuals acting in a vacuum: they acted in the context, and under the impulse, of a past society." *What is History*, 35.

67 Andreski, *Social Sciences as Sorcery*, 22. Andreski poses the issue but claims there is no need to accept the universal determinism doctrine, but that we can explain many phenomena causally, not all are known, and we may indeed discover new ones.

68 Elton, *Practice of History*, 57. Elton is here responding to E.H. Carr's historical philosophy (see 55-58) which posits, according to the former, that "[t]he difference between facts about the past and facts of history hangs upon 'the element of interpretation' which the historian adds to the former in order to create the latter,..." (55).

> Every historian is aware that on occasion he does tamper in all these three ways with what he finds in his authorities. He selects from them what he thinks important, and omits the rest; he interpolates in them things which they do not explicitly say; and he criticizes them by rejecting or amending what he regards as due to misinformation or mendacity.[69]

Lukacs adds to this conversation, somewhat, by writing that "…the historian, as every one of his fellow human beings, should be aware of his limitations. Truth is not given to him. His personal task is, I repeat, the reduction of untruth, and – consequently and simultaneously – the pursuit of truth."[70] Related to these observations is an axiom of the historical method which acknowledges that historians bring their own worldview and predispositions to their own studies of any given subject.[71] Historians ought then to examine their fundamental assumptions. A historian needs, to the best of their ability, to keep their own worldview and personal biases from impinging on their critical and reasonable reconstruction of the sources: a healthy academic environment involving peer review and suggestion is one key way of managing this risk.

The foregoing discussion is one way of conveying that any historical account – whether it be first hand, second hand but contemporary, or later remembrances and accounts based on a harmonization of sources – gives us a presentation of events which, when triangulated with other contemporary accounts, can sometimes give us a fairly solid idea of the main brush strokes in a picture of what really happened, but yet will always remain beyond any measure of strict accuracy in material terms. But history is not a science, and is not interested in strict physical measurements and predictability: history is discipline within the broad category of liberal arts which is most concerned with the idea of communication: and in this specific discipline it is about communicating past evidence about humankind to create a picture of what humans have been and done throughout their history.

Truth, Morality, Laws and the Law

What humans have done throughout their history is also fundamental to any system of law, since it is *a priori* the case that laws have been created *post facto* in regards to the contexts which gave rise to their being engaged in a particular case. The practice of paying deference to precedent is wedded to the idea that, as Shakespeare put so

[69] Collingwood, *Idea of History*, 235.
[70] Lukacs, *Historical Consciousness*, 358.
[71] Robert Jones Shafer, ed., *A Guide to Historical Method*, 3rd ed. (Homewood, Illinois: The Dorsey Press, 1980), 16,18.

eloquently, "...what's past is prologue."[72] Past practice as a guiding principle for future decisions means ideally that law cannot be recklessly capricious but rather must produce outcomes that society has *previously* agreed on as being reasonable pursuant to those people similarly situated before the law. In this sense, moving from one decision connected to the next with slight variations based on the changing mores of society reflected in changing legal instruments makes the growth of legal systems somewhat like a film where every frame is connected to the last one, but is yet slightly different. And yet if you looked at one-hundred of those frames as they appear on raw film you would see very little difference, if at all, from the first to the last, but on the other hand you would see a tremendous difference if you looked at frames that were 10,000 apart from one another. History, on the other hand, is more like a single frame, or a still picture, but those many still pictures, as different as they might be from one another, often give us enough information to make general observations about how similarly situated people, groups, or states have behaved in the past and how they may do so again. As pointed out above, there are many intersecting lines of intent between actors within the legal system and historians.

It is within these intersecting lines of intent and inquiry that we find law and history looking for the same thing, the truth. Law and history are also about referent moralities, evolving moralities, about right and wrong, about justice, and this is so because law and history both are reflections of their concomitant contexts, and thus both speak to their referent ideals, an idea I have explored elsewhere.[73] In the following discussion I interact with the views of historians so as to better understand what one might reasonably expect from historical research in terms of its ability to provide us with 'truth', the touted bellwether of both law and history.

Historians on History

As to the question of whether history teaches us anything beyond 'what people have done and what we are,'[74] it was recognized more than a century ago that very little beyond the common experiences of humankind can be determined from a purely

[72] William Shakespeare, *The Tempest,* act II, scene i, lines 253–54. Antonio is speaking.
[73] C.G. Bateman, "Law as Referent," *Journal Jurisprudence*, vol. 10: *Jurisprudence Today* (Trinity Term, 2011): 225-270.
[74] Paraphrase of Collingwood, *Idea of History*, 10.

historical study. The noted historian James Anthony Froude, in contending that history could never be a science, wrote:

> One lesson, and only one, which history maybe said to repeat with distinctness: that the world is built somehow on moral foundations; that, in the long run, it is well with the good; in the long run, it is ill with the wicked. But this is no science; it is no more that the old doctrine taught long ago by the Hebrew prophets. The theories of M. Comte and his disciples advance us, after all, not a step beyond the trodden and familiar ground. ...So far as those parts of man's doings are concerned, which neither have, nor need have, anything moral about them, so far the laws of him are calculable. ...But pass beyond them, and where are we? In a world where it would be as easy to calculate men's actions by laws like those of positive philosophy as to measure the orbit of Neptune with a foot rule, or weigh Sirius in a grocer's scale.[75]

Froude claimed the impossibility of historical prediction precisely because the moral life of humankind, which was so painfully obvious to all in its good or bad instantiations, was so mixed, even in relation to the smallest variable of an individual human. If humans were consistently selfish, or consistently noble, then you might derive laws, but "so long as the two natures are mixed... so long you will make nothing of [them] except from the old-fashioned moral... point of view."[76] For Froude, the ubiquitous presence of a morality of right and wrong in the human story meant, for instance, that injustice was always and ultimately shown to be overwhelmed by terrible retributive consequences like the French revolutions.[77] While we can see what he meant, that brutal regimes often come to a bitter end, this is hardly consolation for any person or group of people who suffered or are now suffering under such, and Froude does not provide any guarantee or proof that such a regime could not last indefinitely, he relies only on past experience. But many historians discussed herein are perfectly comfortable with these kinds of generalizations as long as they are exactly that: events that are general occurrences in the experience of humankind.

Beyond the observation of a moral component as a lesson derived from the study of history, Froude insists that another lesson history teaches is that we should not sketch out the future based on the past with any kind of certainty we will be correct. He writes:

> Revolutions, reformations, - those vast movements into which heroes and saints have flung themselves, in the belief that they were the dawn of the millennium, - have not borne the fruit which they looked for. ...These great convulsions leave the world changed – perhaps improved, but not improved as the actors in them

[75] Froude, *Science of History*, 456-457.
[76] Ibid., 459.
[77] Ibid., 461.

> hoped it would be. Luther would have gone to work with less heart, could he have foreseen the Thirty Years' War.[78]

Froude's methodology demanded, wherever possible, "[l]et us hear the [historical person] speak, let us see [them] act, and let us be left to form our own opinions about him."[79] For this nineteenth century historian, it was precisely what the historian should not do, telling the readers how to understand the facts beyond the latter's own testimony, which was the most important guiding methodological consideration to be made. Yet Froude's methodology was dependent on an earlier German school of modern historians, and scholar C.H.S. Fifoot pointed out that this idea of letting the historical person speak came from the early nineteenth century German historian Leopold von Ranke, who along with Friedrich Carl von Savigny and Barthold Georg Niebuhr, were the founders of modern history.[80]

> Two dicta of Ranke are of special significance. In the first he proclaimed the true function of the historian: 'not to judge the past or to instruct the present, but merely to show how things actually were.' In the second he indicated his proper technique; he was to build 'not on the accounts of contemporary historians, much less on derivative writers, but on the relations of eye-witnesses and on original documents.' The art of the historian, in effect, was the art of cross-examination, and hearsay evidence was admissible only as secondary and reluctant testimony.[81]

As we will see, though, the idea that 'the facts speak for themselves' was challenged by many later historians such that historians today are expected not only to tell the readers what they interpret the facts to mean, they also must justify it with reasons why their interpretation of those facts should be reasonably believed. But Froude's methodological trajectory of sticking with what we know is a helpful idea reigning in the polemical side of a historian's thought, and while it is true he perhaps asked too much of the 'facts,' his insistence that nothing more than the common experiences of human-kind could be derived from history and that it could never be a science were both ideas taken up a century later by historians such as P.H. Nowell-Smith.

Nowell-Smith pointed out a number of decades ago,[82] that to say that history and the conclusions of historians are not scientifically worked out or proven is not to say that

---

[78] Ibid., 461.
[79] Ibid., 467.
[80] C.H.S. Fifoot, *Law and History in the Nineteenth Century*, Selden Society Lecture, Hall of The Middle Temple, 13 March, 1956 (London: Bernard Quaritch, 1956), 4.
[81] Ibid., 4-5. Here Fifoot was quoting from the prefaces of Ranke's *History of the Romance and Teutonic Peoples* (1824) and *German History in the Reformation Era* (1839).
[82] P.H. Nowell-Smith, *Are Historical Events Unique?*, *Proceedings of the Aristotelian Society*, New Series, vol. 57 (1956-1957).

those same entities are not useful to the human endeavour, by no means. He encouraged us to remember that we learn general truths, in part by reading history, and partly by our own experience: and to demonstrate he noted, "I have no first-hand knowledge of scheming statesmen; but I know some scheming academics."[83] Of the discipline of history, he shows that historians do not make deductions but summaries, that instances of species is not possible in history, that when history uses a generalization they amount to common knowledge, and that generalizations only serve to make other explanations unplausible.[84] W.H. Walsh notes similarly: "[t]he central preoccupation of the historian, there seems no doubt, is not with generalities, but with the precise course of individual events: it is this which he hopes to recount and render intelligible."[85] M.M. Postan had realized this thirty years earlier:

> History, it was thought, could, when suitably employed, not only show up the imperfection of rational propositions but also support general propositions of its own. But the subsequent two or three generations, above all the mid-decades of the Victorian age, taught history yet another lesson. For while the historical school of jurisprudence, Savigny and the rest, found it only too easy to demonstrate the imperfection of the universal principles of rationalist jurisprudence and political theory, they have not been able to replace them with a single historical principle capable of direct general formulation.[86]

Postan also noted that the very subjects of study in history, however general they might appear, all have an individual existence and that the historian always writes what amount to biographies, that is, accounts of single combinations of circumstances.[87] Yet these same combinations of circumstances must be put together in order to reconstruct not general laws inferred from a single instance, but to reconstruct as best we can that single instance. Nowell-Smith concludes, "I ...liken historical explanation to the construction of a jig-saw or pattern into which pieces, the discovered facts, have to be fitted to form what is, in some sense or other, an intelligible whole."[88]

This central idea of an intelligible whole is key to understanding what it is a historian reconstructs with his or her own interpretations of the motives of historical figures based

[83] Nowell-Smith, *Historical Events*, 122. See also Andreski, *Social Sciences*, 9-10.

[84] Nowell-Smith, *Historical Events*, 139. Carr writes that "[j]ust as from the infinite ocean of facts the historian selects those which are significant for his purpose, so from the multiplicity of sequences of cause and effect he extracts those, and only those, which are historically significant; and the standard of historical significance is his ability to fit them into his pattern of rational explanation and interpretation." *What is History?*, 105.

[85] W.H. Walsh, *Philosophy of History: An Introduction*, rev. ed. (New York: Harper Torchbooks, 1967), 39.

[86] M.M. Postan, *The Historical Method in Social Science: An Inaugural lecture* (Cambridge: At the University Press, 1939), 28.

[87] Ibid., 31.

[88] Ibid., 127. See also, D'Arcy, *Meaning and Matter*, 21 & 23; Shafer, *Historical Method*, 6.

on the source materials.[89] These reconstructions and interpretations also require, according to Elton, an imaginative turn in the mind of the historian.[90] He wrote that "the historian must read not only with the analytical eye of the investigator but also with the comprehensive eye of the story-teller. The truth is the product of this double process: understanding what the evidence really says, and understanding how it fits together."[91] Carr similarly notes that historians need an imaginative understanding pursuant to the historical personages they deal with, and yet he warns against having sympathy since that may imply agreement.[92] Collingwood wrote that:

> The historian's picture of his subject, whether that subject be a sequence of events or a past state of things, thus appears as a web of imaginative construction stretched between certain fixed points provided by the statements of his authorities; and if these points are frequent enough and the threads spun from each to the next are construed with due care, always by the *a priori* imagination and never by merely arbitrary fancy, the whole picture is constantly verified by appeal to these data, and runs little risk of losing touch with the reality which it represents.[93]

If we combine the observations of these aforementioned historians, *I suggest that ideally the historian is then using their imagination to re-construct a history based on sources which reads as an intelligible whole.* Further to this, we are also encouraged by historian John Lukacs to keep in mind that "history is thought and spoken and written with words; and the historian must be master of his words as much as of his "facts," whatever those might mean."[94] One can see the integral relationship here between 'imagination' and the historian's use of words: perhaps the latter can be encompassed by the former and assumed to be part of it. Separating the two ideas apart, though, brings it to the front of a historian's mind that when using imagination to re-construct a historical event in an intelligible whole that the reader must be given the most fulsome picture of the event using the words that convey this re-construction most clearly.

---

[89] Cf. Carr, *What is History*?, "What the historian is called on to investigate is what lies behind the act; and to this the conscious thought or motive of the individual actor may be quite irrelevant." (52).

[90] Elton, *Practice of History*, 84. The author concludes that: "Imagination, controlled by learning and scholarship, learning and scholarship rendered meaningful by imagination – these are the tools of enquiry possessed by the historian. He knows that what he is studying is real; he knows that he can never recover all of it and that within his area of recovery the certain, the probable and the speculative will coexist. In short, he knows that the process of historical research and reconstruction will never end, but he is also conscious that this does not render his work unreal or illegitimate." (87).

[91] Ibid.

[92] Carr, *What is History*, 24. In this section he is reviewing Collingwood's outlook and agreeing with this particular aspect of it.

[93] Collingwood, *Idea of History*, 242.

[94] Lukacs, Historical Consciousness, 114.

On the power of language in history and history-making, there are certain key axioms one ought to keep in mind while constructing these "intelligible wholes". It was the General Semantics school, beginning with Alfred Korzybski in 1933, that showed decisively that "[t]he map is *not* the territory it represents…."[95] It only takes a moment of inductive reflection to see how this is absolutely the case. Who will argue that a map of Disneyland is actually Disneyland *itself*? Who will argue that a map of the world is indeed *the* world? Of course, putting it in these terms makes such an observation transcendentally – in the Kantian sense – clear and not susceptible to falsifiability. A later General Semantics writer, S.I. Hayakawa, emphasized this point more lucidly by insisting that "[t]he symbol is NOT the thing symbolized; the word is NOT the thing; the map is NOT the territory it stands for."[96] This is what the historian must keep in mind while creating his own "maps" of past events. When I look at a source document on Constantine, say *Life of Constantine* (*VC*) by Eusebius of Caesarea, the story of that Emperor's rise from a son of one of four Caesar's – the tetrarchy instituted by Diocletian – to the triumphant Christian Emperor is not actually those events at all. They are, at best, abstracted portrayals of Constantine's life based on, if we take Eusebius at his word, a number of sources: "I would be ashamed of myself if I did not put together what I can…."[97] It is clear to modern scholarship that Eusebius cites at least two of his previous works, fifteen legal documents, forty scriptural references, the odd reference to a secular history, and oral testimony from Constantine on some matters.[98] It is evident that Eusebius, having inherited a library and vast learning from Origen of Alexandria,[99] certainly did "put together" a number of sources to construct his story. Seen from the General Semantics perspective, Eusebius was building his own *map* of Constantine's life based on over fifty other maps, and with the exception of his own

---

[95] Alfred Korzybski, *Science and Sanity: An Introduction to Non-Aristotelian Systems and General Semantics*, fourth ed. (Lakeville, Connecticut: The International Non-Aristotelian Library Publishing Company, 1933; 1958), 58.

[96] S.I. Hayakawa, *Language in Thought and Action* (New York: Harcourt, Brace and Company, 1941; 1949), 31. Hayakawa takes "the map is not the territory" directly from the first person to bring General Semantics into the main stream of academia, Alfred Korzybski: Alfred Korzybski, *Science and Sanity: An Introduction to Non-Aristotelian Systems and General Semantics*, fourth ed. (Lakeville, Connecticut: The International Non-Aristotelian Library Publishing Company, 1933; 1958). Korzybski, in turn, apparently [p. 247] took the mapping idea from E.T. Bell, *Numerology* (Baltimore: The Williams & Wilkins company, 1933). Another theory which borrows heavily from this comes from sociologist Edward T. Hall, who suggested the idea of Extension Transference (ET) in which an extension is confused with the process intended: Edward T. Hall, Beyond Culture (Garden City, New York: Anchor Books, 1977), 28-29. Hall does mention Korzybski and Wendell Johnson and predecessors of his who had a similar idea first and were the founders of semantics.

[97] Eusebius of Caesarea, *Eusebius: Life of Constantine*, trans. Averil Cameron and Stuart G. Hall (Oxford: Clarendon Press, 1999), 1.10.1, 71.

[98] Cameron and Hall, *VC*, Intro., 13-24.

[99] For more on the life and influence of Origen on Eusebius, see: C.G. Bateman, *Origen's Role in the Formation of the New Testament Canon* (Thesis (M.C.S.): Regent College, Vancouver, B.C., 2008.), Theological Research Exchange Network (Series) #048-0352: available at SSRN, http://ssrn.com/abstract=1653073.

works, these were all maps constructed by other people – seemingly the most of important of which should have been Constantine's own version of certain events. Eusebius, in the *VC*, leaves to posterity a map of reality, based on a number of other maps, which were themselves, based on other maps of reality. In other words, what Eusebius gives us in the *VC* is not what happened exactly in the actual "life" of Constantine. On the other hand, it is probably the biggest source of information that historians have had access to thus far on the "life" of Constantine. The "General Semantics Boys" – as they are affectionately called sometimes – taught us that being aware of the abstracted nature of documents pretending authority is something akin to a requirement for academics who base their theses on these maps: and historians, least of all, can escape such a duty. So with Lukacs and Berger's suggestions in mind, the historian is to construct a map of history that employs clear and precise language with a foundational tenor of humility in the work which is communicated to the reader by noting at appropriate junctures how tentative are the various pieces of evidence and the very suggestions and conclusions the author wishes to put forth. Great historical work can be an intelligible whole without being conclusive, in fact it must not be, but only suggestive. Even in light of these observations and suggestions from general semantics, there is a great deal to be learned about historical personages and their character and contexts based on the "maps" left to us by their contemporaries.

This aspect of character and context was highlighted by historian's Carr and Collingwood who proposed a seminal technique which, in some form or another, has remained a core element of writing history since: "[h]istory cannot be written unless the historian can achieve some kind of contact with the mind of those about whom he is writing."[100] Collingwood had earlier taken the idea further, claiming that the science of human nature itself can only be done by history, and that in keeping with Locke, the right method for understanding human nature is the historical and plain method.[101] R.G. Collingwood's contribution to the philosophy of history was to make clear a technique which although previously had been sometimes practiced, had not been as popularly emphasized. For Collingwood, history was the history of thought. He wrote:

> The processes of nature can therefore be properly described as sequences of mere events, but those of history cannot. They are not sequences of mere events but processes of actions, which have an inner side, consisting of processes of

---

[100] Carr, *What is History*, 24. John Lukacs writes similarly, "…the motive factors in the history of the world even now ought not to be sought in economic developments as much as within nations and ultimately within the minds and hearts of persons in the midst of nations." Lukacs, *Historical Consciousness*, 212. I think it is clear that Lukacs is referring both to studies of past and present here, and as we know by definition, technically, any study that is taken up is about the past, since as soon as an event is observed it is in the past. It may be more helpful if we think about studies about humans in general as being historical studies *simpliciter*, even if sociology, history, etc. tend to different methods and methodologies.

[101] Collingwood, *Idea of History*, 209.

> thought; and what the historian is looking for is these processes of thought. All history is the history of thought.[102]

For Collingwood this meant a re-thinking of the thoughts of the historical personage under study. Using his famous example of Julius Caesar, he suggests that we not only imagine the actions described concerning the man and Emperor, but that we be able to make suggestions as to what thoughts those were which compelled Caesar to carry out various actions. He claims that all history is a re-enactment of past thoughts, but in the historian's own mind: and the researcher does this by bringing to bear on the problem all their understanding of the particular area, such as 'politics' with Caesar, and he or she must do this in the context of their knowledge and criticize it, judge its value, and correct its errors where they find them.[103]

While Collingwood's direction of re-thinking the thoughts of historical personages to discover the motivations which moved them to act is a bedrock concept in the historical method, he at times seems to move further into metaphysical claims than his baseline idea can bear. He claimed that the historian was concerned with thoughts alone, and that events were only circumstantial to the revealed thoughts.[104] Events are sin qua non to any historian's research, to leave them out of a historical study and examine only thoughts is to move from history to a speculative metaphysical, ethnological, and epistemological research project. In fact, without the subsequent events, the product of Collingwood's antecedent thoughts, we know a priori that we would have never known to look for the thoughts at all. Sometimes in history we know nothing about a personage except for an event they were part of, and thus to construct their thoughts with only the event as contextual data would be speculative.

John Lukacs' historical philosophy was claimed to be in this "thought" line of Collingwood's, but Lukacs attempts to separate himself from this most influential of the historical philosophers. Lukacs wrote, "[f]or Collingwood, with all of the important recognitions of his idea of history, could not quite liberate himself from his inherited positivism."[105] Lukacs offers what he accords as proof of this in claiming that Collingwood's focus on the inside of events, the thoughts of the actors, is too narrow an explanation and Lukacs instead insists that the historian see the world in two ways,

102 Ibid., 215.

103 Ibid.

104 Ibid., 217.

105 Lukacs, *Historical Consciousness*, 351-352. Lukacs may be right that in claiming Collingwood inherited some positivist tendencies, which the latter admits to fighting against (*Idea of History*, 228), but ironically even Lukacs himself was prone to this in his categorization of 'important' versus 'significant' events – even though he claims "It is not my purpose to establish categories for a classification of events. All such categories leak. Historical life is infinitely stronger and richer than historical theory." (131). Yet, disavowing oneself from 'categorizing' when that is precisely what he did is somewhat misleading, and perhaps dulls his own criticism of Collingwood, who came before him, for doing the same thing.

"from the outside in and from the inside out – and both of these experiences and thoughts occur simultaneously."[106] I do not think, if given the chance to answer this charge, that Collingwood would deny the obvious symbiotic relationship between the inside and outside of an event – the fact that he first gave his novel idea the appellations he did is instructive on this point – but rather that the historian's main task was not the 'what' of an event but the much more instructive 'why'. Everyone is given the 'what' in the extant evidence, yet it is only the gifted historian who can imaginatively reconstruct the 'why'.

Collingwood himself points to the limitations of an historian's mind wherein historical matter may be unintelligible in some cases. Collingwood writes:

> It may thus be said that historical inquiry reveals to the historian the powers of his own mind. Since all he can know historically is thoughts that he can re-think for himself, the fact of his coming to know them shows him that his mind is able (or by the very effort of studying them has become able) to think in these ways. And conversely, whenever he finds certain historical matters unintelligible, he has discovered a limitation of his own mind; he has discovered that there are certain ways in which he is not, or no longer, or not yet, able to think.[107]

And yet Collingwood's overreaching speculations must not crowd out the very seminal tool that he emphasized as his main thesis: that historians would do better not to merely describe historical events or repeat what historical personages are alleged to have done, which we have evidence for, but instead to get behind the events, to get *inside* them – to use his word – to suggest what thoughts and motivations likely moved Caesar, for instance, to make the decision to cross the Rubicon. Contrary to any inference one might take from Luckas' claim that the more senior historian still adhered to positivism, Collingwood stated he was engaged in a running fight against a positivist conception of history that treated events as a scientist would handle natural events:[108] and so we can re-think Collingwood's thoughts, and find here one of them which goes some way to explaining the historical event of his fight against the positivist influence in history in his book, *The Idea of History*.

Also engaged in a fight against positivism was Lukacs himself in his most important monograph, *Historial Consciousness*. His main point was that beyond the fact that complete objectivity is impossible and deceiving, that inherent in looking at history as a form of thought was the condition that the history of everything may not only be the explanation of it but also that "the historical description of an idea amounts to that idea, *impure et*

[106] Ibid., 352.
[107] Collingwood, *Idea of History*, 218.
[108] Ibid., 228.

complexe."[109] This historian insisted that a consciousness of history demands the rejection of determinism, whether objective or subjective, and further necessitates a recognition of historical knowledge as personal and participant.[110] He clarifies this somewhat by writing:

> It is not only that in history the observer and the observed belong to the same species: It is that the kind of understanding which is – or rather, should be – required of the historian inevitably involves a kind of sympathetic participation in the person or persons, in the lives and in the minds, in which he is interested, and which he will attempt to describe.[111]

Burckhardt before him, Lukacs admits, first suggested that the interest of the historian needs to be personal, authentic, and participatory.[112] So as Lukacs seems to have taken his cue with the phrase and idea of an evolving "historical consciousness" from Collingwood,[113] and then his idea of participant knowledge from Burckhardt, he himself finds himself in the evolving stream of his own historical consciousness and thus any criticism of Collingwood's ideas are muted by the manifest debt Lukacs owes to the former, which he seems to finally agree with, at least in part.[114]

The historical method being discussed herein aims for nothing less than such a standard: *this standard requires an imaginative re-construction of an historical event and its concomitant personages which is, clearly, based on extant data, but which also must engage in a participatory re-thinking of the characters involved such that the end result can be read as an intelligible whole.* Now, while with Froude and Nowell-Smith we can claim that history is not science, we still understand how these suggestive, intelligible, historical studies can provide us with useful information about how similarly situated human beings acted in the past and therefore might do so again.[115]

Again, historians are attempting not only the "what" of history, but as we have witnessed in the words of many influential historians, there is a germane focus on the "why". Why did an event happen in one way instead of another? Further, because we have recorded

---

109 Lukacs, *Historical Consciousness*, 324-325.
110 Ibid., 325.
111 Ibid., 355.
112 Ibid.
113 Ibid., 45. Lukacs quotes Collingwood as writing: "…It is only when a man's historical consciousness has reached a certain point of maturity that he realizes how different have been the ways in which different sets of people have thought." Lukacs cites this as being on p age 86 of *The Idea of History*, but it is not, it actually comes from R.G. Collingwood, *An Essay on Metaphysics*, ed. Rex Martin (Oxford: Oxford University Press, 1940; 1998; 2002), 56.
114 Lukacs, *Historical Consciousness*, 352. Lukacs does this in a footnote unfortunately and closes his criticism of him with the observation of another scholar. J. O'Connell, "R.G. Collingwood: The Historical Dimensions of Consciousness," *To-Wards* (Los Angeles, Winter 1980-1981).
115 Carr, *What is History*, 37. "Great history is written precisely when the historian's vision of the past is ulluminated by insights into the problems of the present." (37).

an instantiation in some broad category of events, such as political revolutions, why did the event happen at all? Asking "what are the human actions and motivations which caused the event" is similar to asking 'why'. I might suggest that every discipline has its generally accepted *what* – science has "matter", philosophy has "ideas", etc., and not all of these datum are mutually exclusive to their discipline – and that for history our *what* is human actions resulting in events. Similar to scientists applying formula and technique to their matter in order to come up with physical laws, historians must engage in a critical analysis of the recorded actions of historical figures in order to suggest, not laws, but explanations of the probable motivations which best explain the actions of these people in light of other historical examples and the common experiences of human kind, including our own experience.[116] History, as Marc Bloch rightly noted, is aiming towards the beacon light of understanding,[117] and asking both the "what" and "why" questions brings us closer to achieving this goal.

Historical Method

> It often seems to me as if History was like a child's box of letters, with which we can spell any word we please.

[116] See generally P.H. Nowell-Smith, *Are Historical Events Unique?*, *Proceedings of the Aristotelian Society*, New Series, vol. 57 (1956-1957): 107-160. Nowell-Smith makes a number of interesting observations germane to the question of historical events and entities, a few of which I will note here: "…despotism, the bourgeoisie and the Holy Roman Empire are all entities." (140); "…historians use general words, and the use of such words presupposes the recognition of similarities. To talk of the Revolutions of 1688, 1789, and 1848 is already to recognize these events as similar in some respects." [And yet for the historian who studies the Revolution of 1688, he recognizes there is no such thing as a typical revolution.] (117); "Explanation in history often takes the form, not of discovering the events with which a given event is causally connected in the regularity sense, but in expounding in detail in what the given event consisted." (135); "What plays a part of an experiment in science is provided, in history, by the discovery of new evidence." (157); "Explanation of a fact takes the form of fitting it into a picture. Does the fact to be explained fit better into this picture or into that?" (138); "…historians actually proceed by studying the original documents which mostly consist of contemporary written evidence; and to understand these just is to think in the language and style of the authors. This may be difficult – I have nowhere pretended that the study of history is easy-; but if there is any mystery about it, we shall have to rest content with the fact that history is mysterious." (158); "It is only in the end that the Diffusionist [diffusion of ideas versus a common realization by peoples of different cultures without diffusion of practices or beliefs] appeals to generalizations, and then only to those of the large, inarticulate, common-sense sort; the Evolutionist treats generalizations, perhaps one day to be subsumed under a theory, as his goal. The one is an historian; the other, perhaps, a scientist." (160).

[117] Bloch, *Historian's Craft*, 143.

† Froude, *Science of History*, 443.

†† Elton, *Practice of History*, 74.

James Anthony Froude, *The Science of History*†

I often wonder what the illustrious dead make of all the things historians discover about them; if the Elysian fields ring with Homeric laughter, a continued interest in historical writing may well be the cause.

G.R. Elton, *The Practice of History*††

Truth may be stranger than fiction, but we know from the grotesque ideological fabrications within the last hundred years, for which, seemingly, whole societies have fallen for, that fiction can oftentimes cause more harm than truth. With this thought in mind we acknowledge from the outset that the historian and their method aim at discovering the truth about the past and at no time, ideally, will they purposely assume the role of 'historian of the gaps.' Elton notes that the historical method is both a cure for the two uncertainties of the historian, the lack of knowledge and the need to select, and it is further designed to protect them against their "human difficulties," which it often does.[118] Thus, perhaps, this is why Collingwood answers the question of what history is as "'for' human self-knowledge. …the only clue to what man can do is what man has done. The value of history, then, is that it teaches us what man has done and thus what man is."[119] The whole of the historical method is governed by the "first principle of historical understanding, namely that the past must be studied in its own right, for its own sake, and on its own terms."[120]

---

118 Ibid., 63. On the historical method, Elton writes interestingly: "Two fairly common attitudes to historical research and method have done something to give the dog a bad name. On the one hand, there are the 'methodologists' who make a a laborious and tedious science out of the historian's techniques, teaching it (as in some American graduate courses) almost as an independent discipline. On the other, we have the remaining inspired amateurs (this is an English failing) to whom the study of evidence presents no problems that cannot be solved by the common sense available to any reasonably intelligent [person]. Neither attitude has much to recommend it. The first turns a necessary tool into a nightmare mystery and is liable to produce egg-bound history or no history at all; the second promotes the exercise of prejudice and dilettantism, and is liable to produce pointless ephemera." (64).

119 Collingwood, *Idea of History*, 10.

120 Ibid., 65. Related to this, according to Elton, are two fundamental principles expressed as questions: "exactly what evidence is there, and exactly what does it mean? Knowledge of all the sources, and competent criticism of them – these are the basic requirements of a reliable historiography." He later writes, "There is a single question which the researcher must ask himself in assessing his evidence: how and why did this come into existence? From the historian's point of view, all evidence divides into two kinds: that produced specifically for his attention, and that produced for some other purpose." (77). A laudable example of this would be the difference in the Christian New Testament between Christian literature, books such as Hebrews and Revelation, and Paul's genuine letters, such as Romans and 1

According to Gustavson, there are basic characteristics of historical inquiry: natural curiosity about what is underneath an event; looking to the past for origins, relationships, and comparisons to solve our problems; examination of societies' dynamic forces; the genuine continuity of events; the genuine process of change; the willingness to abandon preconceived hopes and humble ourselves at the feet of the reality we find; and finally that historians recognize all events as unique.[121] These considerations are central to a sound historical method – also keeping in mind the obvious need recognized by Elton for historical scholarship to rest on "a broad-fronted attack upon all the relevant material"[122] – and even though they could be implemented along with the instrumentalization of a variety of methodologies as opposed to method, and keeping in mind the aforementioned warning for historians to be aware of their own pre-concieved ideas and agendas, it seems that it would be much better to leave methodological perspectives and their concomitant aims to one side when constructing descriptions of historical events and their attendant personalities. Of course, after the history has been re-constructed into a suggestion of how and why events happened, then methodology might be useful for a historian who wants to then suggest why a given event became historically important to some specified group in society which relates to their methodological concerns. For instance, Martin Luther King's March on Washington can be re-constructed quite accurately employing the historical method, but it also instructs the methodological concerns of scholars who want to explain, using their own critical methodology as a guide, the "whys and hows," of the evolving story of African-American peoples in the history of the United States. Yet, when re-constructing the March on Washington itself as an event with its concomitant personages, it is the historical method rather than any methodology which will keep a historian's research trajectory as close to objective as possible.[123] In other words, and as the fundamental

Corinthians. The former were written with the implicit intent to furnish future generations with an account of what happened, and the latter were written to specific groups of people in a that single historical context with no thought of the future. On this particular topic, see G. Adolf Deissmann, *Bible Studies: Contributions Chiefly from Papyri and Inscriptions to the History of the Language, the Literature, and the Religion of Hellenistic Judaism and Primitive Christianity*, trans. Alexander Grieve, 2nd ed. (Edinburgh: T. & T. Clark, 1903). For instance, Deissmann writes: "Certain as it seems to the author that the authentic messages of Paul are letters, he is equally sure that we have also a number of epistles from New Testament times. They belong, as such, to the beginnings of "Christian literature". The author considers the Letter to the Hebrews as most unmistakable of all an epistle." (49). Deissmann also writes elsewhere, ". . . the contrast in which the Epistle to the Hebrews, for instance, stands linguistically to the earlier texts of Primitive Christianity, is peculiarly instructive to us. It points to the fact that the Epistle to the Hebrews, with its more definitely artistic, more literary language (corresponding to its more theological subject-matter), constituted an epoch in the history of the new religion. Christianity is beginning to lay hands on the instruments of culture; the literary and theological period has begun." G. Adolf Deissmann, *Light from the Ancient East: The New Testament Illustrated by Recently Discovered Texts of the Graeco-Roman World*, trans. Lionel R. M. Strachan, rev. and enl. ed. (Grand Rapids: Baker Book House, 1978), 70-71.

121 Gustavson, *A Preface*, 6-7.

122 Elton, Practice of History, 66.

123 Nowell-Smith, *Historical Events*, 155-156.

axiom of historical research in context, it is both the evidence for the events themselves as well as the ideas and motivations in the minds of the historical actors that are most important to producing the intelligible whole we seek after.

The historical method, as alluded to above, is also very aware of social forces which change the course of history. Generally these forces are under the rubrics of economic, religious, technological, institutional, ideological, and military forces.[124] When looking, for example, as I do at Constantine and the Christian Church, all these forces figure into the interpretation of the one historical figure and one historical institution and their specific relationship. The economy of the Empire was very unstable prior to Constantine's ascension to power and the Christian Church was a formidable and organized social force across his Empire. Technology had probably the least influence as a social force at this time, but the network of Roman roads that had been built throughout the Empire insured that Christianity would spread that much faster and also insured that edicts, decretals, and letters from the Emperor to his subjects would reach them much faster than otherwise. The institutional and bureaucratic nature of the Christian Church and its stabilizing potential for the emperor's unstable empire was recognized by Constantine and adopted largely for this reason: this seminal suggestion was first made by nineteenth century historian Jacob Burckhardt.[125] The ideology of Christianity, in contrast to the pagan pantheon of gods, was one where even the poorest of society could become members, and the message of the Church was international in outlook, not limited to a single state or class of people: it was more expansive in nature. [126] The Greeks had gods for the Greeks, the Romans for the Romans, even though we know that these gods were imported by the latter from the former. It was not until the Severan dynasty (193-235) ruled the Empire that the Syrian influence of a single god began to take root in Roman society, and with it the idea that god's from one region could be adopted in another. Such a transformation set the stage for Constantine's

---

124 Gustavson, *A Preface*, 52: see generally 24-52.

125 Jacob Burckhardt, *The Age of Constantine the Great*, trans. by Moses Hadas (New York: Doubleday Anchor Books, 1956).

126 Michael Lipka, *Roman Gods: A Conceptual Approach* (Leiden: Brill, 2009), 187-188. Lipka writes, "It was the spatial independence that gave the Christian and Jewish gods an advantageous position: first, it made them virtually impregnable and 'immune' to imperial intervention. Since the Jewish and Christian gods were not spacially bound, their cult was elusive and beyond the control of Roman officialdom. Second, such independence made the Christian and Jewish gods extremely marketable merchandises that could easily be accommodated to virtually any environment without further expense. The latter point was reinforced by the monotheistic character of the two gods, allowing their export virtually anywhere without the necessity to accommodate their functions (naturally, a single god was functionally indifferent). In fact, in their striking lack of spatial focalization and functional self-sufficiency the Christian and Jewish gods were the only 'international gods' of the ancient world, the gods, as pointedly remarked by Weber, favoured by "itinerant journeyman", (Weber, Economy, 512) or in the words of Ando, "in ambition a truly imperialist cult." (Ando, 2007, 445) It was not until Constantine the Great that the Christian concept of god began to be formed by spacial foci."

adoption of the one God of Christianity, the Roman world by then having already become familiar with this kind of societal adoption.

One can see then, how all these *forces* figure into reconstructing any kind of suggestive intelligible whole of the relationship between Constantine and the Christian Church. What caused Constantine to choose to adopt the Christian Church as his own and for his Empire? This is a question that can produce a variety of answers, but it highlights one of the main problems for historians, explaining the causes of historical events. Gustavson enumerates a number of questions which may help narrow down this investigation. These questions ask the level of significance for any possible immediate cause, victorious principles and their provenance, strengths and weaknesses of personalities, new ideology, perspectives of economic groups, religious forces, role of technology, institutional strengths and weaknesses, and finally whether the physical environment played a role in the events.[127] As one can see, causation is here intertwined with the social forces, but in most cases it could not be otherwise. Some of these considerations may or may not be applicable to a given historical reconstruction but in the main these are questions that historians must grapple with. If an event has a multiplicity of causes, which covers just about every single one, then one helpful way of deciding which are the most important is by asking the question: if one of the factors under consideration were left out, let's say if Christianity did not exist in the organized and ubiquitous way it did in Constantine's time, would the event outcome have been different or even happened at all?[128] One can see how very quickly even a rough sketch of which factors were more causally relevant could be reached by using such a method.

When a historical event takes place, change takes place. Historically, events are also always connected to continuities by their dependent and antecedent instantiations. What is usually referred to as "Change and Continuity"[129] is a necessary part of a historian's suggestive reconstruction of the evidence to explain a particular historical event. If I claim that Constantine both changed the organization and laws of the Empire and was also in vigorous continuity with Rome's past traditions and practices, I would be right on both counts. In history, change and continuity are axiomatic to any explanation of events, there are rarely such things as completely new beginnings or clean breaks with the past, but they do occur.[130] As E.P. Cheyney wrote, "[a]ctual origins elude us; everything is the outcome of something preceding… the immediate, sudden appearance

[127] Burckhardt, *Constantine*, 62.

[128] Ibid., 63.

[129] Shafer, Historical Method, 19-21; Gustavson, *A Preface*, 65-80.

[130] Daniel Philpott points to such a break when writing on the Westphalian Peace and its break with the past pursuant the history of the sovereign state : "In history, perfect fissures are rare, but as historical faults go, Westphalia is as clean as they come." Daniel Philpott, *On the Cusp of Sovereignty: Lessons from the Sixteenth Century, Sovereignty at the Crossroads?, Morality and International Politics in the Post-Cold War Era*, ed. Luis E. Lugo (Lanham, Maryland: Rowman & Littlefield Publishers, 1996), 43.

of something, its creation by an individual or a group at some one moment in time, is unknown in history."[131] Marc Bloch noted "...for most historical realities the very notion of a starting-point remains singularly elusive."[132] While events are connected to their past by definition, it is also true that some events are such radical departures from past practice as to become historical markers for the beginning of a new era in history. I argue that the marriage of Church and State under Constantine, with its concomitant and subsequent alteration of the constitution and laws of the Empire and realignment of the balance of powers, was one of these markers.

Ideal Forms, Necessary Assumptions, and a Legal Historian's Canon

The Greek word κανόν (canon) means a straight rod, or measuring device which is used as a standard to measure the quality of something against a perfectly straight rule.[133] Canon also refers to a collection of writings, and in the historical method suggested here, both definitions are applicable. We have seen how important the contributions of Burckhart, Collingwood, Carr, Bloch, Elton, and others from the ranks of historians have been in the sounding out of a reliable historical method, and thus their seminal works on method have been highlighted in the foregoing and are part of my historian's canon. Yet we also see that the insights of philosophers and sociologists, like Whitehead and Berger, also give us a more stable view of what history actually is and thus suggesting the kinds of questions, inquiries, and answers the historian may reasonably hope to offer up. What follows is a contemplation of other stabilizing ideas found in the seminal works of scholars in a variety of fields including science, anthropology, and philosophy. These are also part of my historian's canon, and bear directly on the way I approach historical evidence. In terms of the idea of Canon as straight rod, rule, or measuring device, the measuring device here is the method discussed herein, and what historians measure is the evidences they rely on in fashioning their reconstructions of past events, and importantly the very reconstructions themselves.

---

131 E.P. Cheyney, *Law in History and Other Essays* (New York, 1927), 11. As in Gustavson, *A Preface*, 63-64.
132 Bloch, *Historian's Craft*, 29.
133 Walter Bauer, *A Greek-English Lexicon of the New Testament and other Early Christian Literature*, Third Edition, Fredrick William Danker et al. eds. (Chicago: University of Chicago Press, 2000), 507-508; A further definition reads: A bar, "... esp. to keep a thing straight [such as] ...staves which preserved the shape of the shield," Henry George Liddell and Robert Scott, *A Greek-English Lexicon*, Sir Henry Stuart Jones and Roderick McKenzie, eds. (Oxford: Clarendon Press, 1996), 875.

We return to Whitehead for a stepping off point in the following discussion pertaining to the completion of my historian's canon. Whitehead wrote: "[t]he safest general characterization of the European philosophical tradition is that it consists of a series of footnotes to Plato."[134] Here Whitehead does two things for this argument, the most important being the admission that Plato's accounting of Socrates and his own philosophy has shaped every philosophical idea since in the European tradition, including historical study. The second observation is connected to the first and amounts to the acknowledgement of the dependent nature of knowledge in general, and for historians their reconstructions of historical events and persons are indubitably dependent for the obvious reason that it is only through the works of chroniclers, other historical documents, and physical evidence that we know anything at all about the past.

In terms of Plato's philosophy, we see a dependency emerging immediately in the works of Aristotle, the student of Plato, and using Whitehead's nomenclature, we have the first set of footnotes to Plato, as it were. Almost everything Aristotle postulated was a response or an extension of Plato, and he writes of his teacher Plato and "the old man" Socrates in his work more than any other thinkers of Classical Greece. Just as Plato cited Socrates in identifying the major influence behind the philosophy found in Plato's works, so Aristotle is not shy about giving proper credit to Plato as his progenitor, even if the former's philosophy evolved into a categorically different system than his mentor's. In some sense, though, they could have hardly done otherwise. Here was a small group of wealthy Greek men who could afford a leisurely life of learning. The world of the 'academy', literally, was much smaller and more conspicuous then, but it is from this small group that we get the beginnings of the Western tradition of epistemology, the study of how we know what we claim to know.

Socrates, at his own trial, gave colour to one of the ideas the modern historical method holds most dear, humility before the evidence and the jettisoning of our own pre-conceived assumptions about "what happened". Right at the very beginning of Plato's account of the trial of Socrates, you have the accused defending himself and answering the charge of Meletus and Anytus that he was teaching the young not to believe in the gods and instead some other spiritual truth, thus corrupting the young. Socrates knew that his reputation was based on having "a certain kind of wisdom:"[135] but, Socrates asked the court, what did this really amount to?[136] We read that Socrates had learned from a friend[137] who had consulted the Oracle at Delphi pursuant to the question of whether anyone was wiser than Socrates: the Pythian answered that no one was wiser

---

134 Whitehead, Process and Reality, 2.1, 607.

135 Plato, *Apology*, *Plato: Complete Works*, trans. G.M.A. Grube, ed. John M. Cooper (Indianapolis/Cambridge: Hackett Publishing Company, 1997), 20.d, 21

136 Plato, *Apology*, Cooper, 20.e-23.b, 21-22.

137 Ibid., 21.a, 21. The friend is identified as Chaerephon, who happened to be deceased at the time of the trial but who many knew, and whose brother could corroborate the event.

than Socrates. Socrates concluded that what the god meant was that "[t]his man among you, mortals, is wisest who, like Socrates, understands that his wisdom is worthless."[138] Of course Socrates is recognized elsewhere by Plato as the wisest man that he ever knew,[139] and even Socrates himself relates that his wisdom was above many that he interviewed, but specifically with the proviso that his wisdom comes from his acknowledgment of his lack of it.[140] Herein begins the tradition in epistemology generally, which found its way into the historical method, of openly acknowledging what one does not know for certain instead of pretending, as the interviewees of Socrates did – Politicians, Poets, etc. – authoritative wisdom on a given subject.

While Socrates and Plato are not thought of as historians per se, there are significant portions of Plato's dialogues which are essentially written *as* history: notwithstanding the fact that myth is often interwoven in what were oral accounts of the generations that preceded their own.[141] While the historical passages are important in and of themselves, there is something closer to the teleological, cosmological, and ontological centre of Socrates and Plato's ideas which I would like to focus on briefly, as it relates to the study of the past. The theory of Forms[142] which emerges from the postulations and suggestions of the aforementioned philosophers consists of two axioms: first, ideal forms are a necessary condition for the existence of lower forms of reality. For instance, the ideal Form of "horse", perfect in every aspect of horse-ness, allows for the less perfect beings that are significantly like this ideal Form to pass in the physical world as horses. The second axiom concerning the Forms is that they are only perceivable by the human mind. George Klosko writes of Plato's Forms, "[a]t heart, the theory of Forms concerns absolute, timeless, immutable essences, completely removed from the sensible world. Because they can be perceived only by the mind, Plato locates them in the 'intelligible realm.'"[143] I suggest that these aspects of (a) existentially immutable and (b) existentially realized in the mind, pursuant to the Forms, are both related to the study of history. The existentially immutable quality of the Forms, being almost frozen in time and space, is exactly how we find history: in other words, what happened in the past is simply what happened, there is no changing it. It is as if each moment in the past is

---

138 Ibid., 23.a-23.b, 22; 21.b-21.e, 21.

139 Plato, *Phaedo*, trans. G.M.A. Grube, ed. Cooper, 1997, 118.a, 100.

140 Plato, *Apology*, Cooper, 21.a-21.e, 21.

141 If Plato's *Apology* is not written history, then nothing is. It is Plato's account of the trial of Socrates based on multiple eye-witness accounts from mutual friends of both men. As for other examples in Plato's works, there are a number. The cosmological explanation of mankind's development in *Statesman* and *Timaeus*, and a partial Athenian history about their war with the Atlantian culture in the *Timaeus* and *Critias*, serve as two ready and familiar examples. A for the interweaving of myth and oral history, everyone Herodotus and especially Homer were engaging in the same practice, hardly discounting any similar tendency we may find in Plato.

142 For a concise discussion of the Forms, see: George Klosko, *The Development of Plato's Political Theory*, 2nd ed. (New York: Oxford, 2006): 87-92.

143 Ibid., 88.

frozen in time and space, forever remaining what it was at the moment in history it was realized. The other aspect of the Forms which makes them only accessible to the mind is very much related to the reconstructions of history which are postulated by historians. When we read Gibbon's account of the fall of the Roman Empire the reader might be led to believe that his story is *the* story which actually happened, but it certainly is not.

What Gibbon wrote about the fall of the Roman Empire was his interpretation of a multitude of relevant sources into a coherent story which existed in his mind and was transferred to paper by his pen. In some manner of speaking, then, on the one hand we have the actual history – the ideal Form – of Rome's fall which is what happened on a moment by moment basis to that Empire over the course of some twelve-hundred plus years[144] but which is now only a fact *in* the past and not a fact *from* the past: and on the other hand we have the great historian Edward Gibbon's reconstruction in writing of that past which, based on the vast amount of extant evidence we have from Roman history, leads us to suggest that his work is very likely "Fall-of-Romeness-like" enough to give it the name of an account of the fall of Rome. While Gibbon's account is not the ideal Form in its being the very history itself, we are still well within reason to name it according to its form, the *Decline and Fall of the Roman Empire*. The observation here is that if the reconstruction of an historical event is enough like the ideal Form – the nature of which is unchanging, and by definition it must be – then we are justified in seeing those historical interpretations of the past as being reliable only to the degree that their attributes are close enough to the little we do know about the ideal Form to deserve being put under such a rubric. M.M. Postan commented on this inability to reach perfection by writing:

> For the uncertainty of historical results is due not to their being produced by historians, but to their being based on social facts. …And if I personally am hopeful about the contribution of history, it is because I am not hopeless about the task of social science. The reason why I am not hopeless is perhaps due to the fact that I am not overly ambitious. I do not believe that the science of society will ever achieve the perfection of astronomy, but neither do I think that scientific thought is impossible or useless on lower ranges of perfection.[145]

The predictive certainty of science is not the aim of history, rather history aims at certain events to suggest as complete a picture of that event and its personages as possible. Similarly to what Postan said in his lecture concerning scientific thought, information on a single event or person amongst the lower forms does not make it useless. In fact, the historian's reconstruction is often as close as we are ever going to get to the ideal form, that is, unless another historian after them reconstructs the event with more evidence.

---

144 Gibbon began his history with the year 180 CE.

145 Postan, *Historical Method in Social Science*, 36.

This is a question of the relationship between a historian's interpretation and historical evidence, as Carr puts it:

> The relation between the historian and his facts is one of equality, of give-and-take. As any working historian knows, if he stops to reflect what he is doing as he thinks and writes, the historian is engaged on a continuous process of moulding his facts to his interpretation and his interpretation to his facts. It is impossible to assign primacy to one over the other.
>
> The historian starts with a provisional selection of facts, and a provisional interpretation in the light of which that selection has been made – by others as well as himself. As he works, both the interpretation and the selection and ordering of facts undergo subtle and perhaps partly unconscious changes, through the reciprocal action of one or the other. …My first answer therefore to the question 'What is history?' is that it is a continuous process of interaction between the historian and his facts, and unending dialogue between the present and the past.[146]

Now, for historians, then, actual history itself is our ideal Form, and as such while it is accessible to us via the instrumentality of our minds applied to source evidence, history itself remains irretrievable in the same way Plato's ideal Forms were. This seems like a serious limit on its effectiveness from an epistemological standpoint, and yet in the same way a variety of horse-like creatures are sufficiently similar to be identified as close enough to the ideal form of horse to *be* a horse, so with enough historical data about a person or event involving persons, we can fairly identify a historian's thoughtful re-construction of the data in terms such as, for instance, 'the life of Julius Caesar' or 'the Punic Wars'. The observation of history as its own ideal form on its face, once through the looking glass of this philosophical metaphor, seems straight forward enough, but its employment here is only to set the boundaries for a historical method that is grounded in what is possible given our perspective. As Kierkegaard pointed out:

> Philosophy is perfectly right in saying that life must be understood backward. But then one forgets the other clause – that it must be lived forward. The more one thinks through this clause, the more one concludes that life in temporality never becomes properly understandable, simply because never at any time does one get perfect repose to take a stance – backward.[147]

This is very much to the point, we never get the ability to have a backward stance because we – and that includes historians – live our lives going forward. While our

[146] Carr, *What is History*, 29-30.

[147] Søren Kierkegaard, JP I 1030 (Pap. IV A 164) n.d., 1843, *The Essential Kierkegaard*, eds. Howard V. Hong and Edna H. Hong (Princeton: Princeton University Press 2000) p. 12.

understanding of life depends and is benefitted on our memories and the observations and evidence of others in the past, we never have "what happened" fully or properly in our grasp. Again, this is navigational information for the historian, it is about immovable boundaries beyond which no one may claim certainty, but this side of which historians reconstruct the evidence we do possess into suggestions about past societies and peoples, and these responsible reconstructions provide us with enough of an edifice to say that we are fully justified in taking their proposals seriously. The degree to which a historian presents a reconstruction which is reasonable vis-à-vis our shared human experiences and brought to bear in the interpretive process on the source data is the degree to which we will provisionally accept their suggestions.

It is with Plato, then, that we begin our journey into the metaphysical realm, so to speak, as we try and reconstruct things we have not witnessed, experienced, or in most cases ever lived through. This practice, dubious as it may sound described this way, is at the heart of what the historian does, and as pointed out above it also applies to legal actors in our modern context who are reconstructing events to get at the 'truth' of the matter, in order to achieve as just an outcome as possible. The historian's just outcome, on the other hand, is not to arrive at a certain 'justice' per se, unless written as polemics, but is rather an inquiry seeking only to explain what happened and why based on the motivations of the actors at issue. In its essence, the historical reconstruction process is a metaphysical exercise, since for the historian it is beyond them precisely because it is behind them, as Kierkegaard alluded to. Yet, even in light of this, we are also inextricably connected to the ideas and lives of historical figures such as King Josiah, Jesus of Nazereth, Joan of Arc, Abraham Lincoln, Harriet Beecher Stowe, Martin Luther King Jr., and Ghandi for the very simple reason that we are all people in the same sense they were and, just as importantly, that we are also born within the further evolution of the social realities in which all past peoples have created, not merely the ones that have been made famous given our preferences and predilections. The most important part of this evolution of human culture and practice for me as a historian is that we as people are the ones who have decided to, and continue to, create the social realities that both bind us together and in many cases separate us: either in the singular (me vis-à-vis you) or the plural (us vis-à-vis them). This fundamental axiom which imbues history has been most singularly noted by sociologist Peter Berger.

Peter Berger made clear, admittedly with the observations of many other scholars in hand, that our social reality is one we construct ourselves.[148] Humankind constructs its social reality, and this is related to how historians reconstruct versions of the Form-

[148] Berger and Luckmann, *The Social Construction of Reality*, 1966: Berger and Luckmann point to three main "activities" of humankind in their social construction of reality. Externalization is ongoing in human activity, objectification is the naming of things, and internalization is the adoption of the activities and meanings one is confronted with. (49); Peter L. Berger, *The Sacred Canopy: Elements of a Sociological Theory of Religion* (Garden City, New York: Doubleday, 1967).

reality of the past based on any evidence they have for those various reconstructions. Berger is the creator of a concept he named "nomos" which simply stands for a meaningful order created by a group of people. Berger writes:

> It may now be understandable if the proposition is made that the socially constructed world is, above all, an ordering of experience. A meaningful order, or nomos, is imposed upon the discrete experiences and meanings of individuals. [*] To say that society is a world-building enterprise is to say that it is ordering, or nomizing, activity.[149]

In a manner of speaking then, Berger becomes his own "creator" of social reality by constructing the idea of *nomos* to make clearer the way in which people constantly create and adopt their own constructions of reality. For historians, Berger's suggestions prove useful on more than one level, and they certainly strengthen the historical method's insistence that one be as familiar with the *nomos* of the historical figure/s involved in a study before we begin to suggest what may have motivated them to act as they did. Carr similarly points out that "[a]s soon as we are born, the world gets to work on us and transforms us from merely biological into social units. Every human being at every stage of history of pre-history is born into a society and from his earliest years is moulded by that society."[150] This kind of moulding, ordering, and nomizing activity is concomitant in the story of humankind. To take a stark historical example of 'nomos' directly from the Christian Church of the Middle Ages, the *nomos* for Thomas Aquinas was a meaningful order that allowed the burning of non-Roman Catholic Christians precisely because those latter Christians refused to adopt the *nomos* created by the former. The answer to why people of the day did not raise a protest is that the *nomos* of the Roman Catholic Church of the Middle Ages which Aquinas et al. inherited was one built in large part on the ideas of Augustine who planted the seeds of indifference to violence by writing, for instance:

> And he [The Bishop/Judge[151] of the state] thinks it no wickedness that innocent witnesses are tortured regarding the crimes of which other men are accused; or that the accused are put to the torture, so that they are often overcome with anguish, and, though innocent, make false confessions regarding themselves, and are punished; or that, though they be not condemned to die, they often die during, or in consequence of, the torture. ... These numerous and important

[149] Peter Berger, *The Sacred Canopy,* 19. * Berger notes: "[t]he term "nomos" is indirectly derived from Durkheim by, as it were, turning around his concept of *anomie.* The latter was first developed in his *Suicide* (Glencoe, Ill.: Free Press, 1951), 192."

[150] Carr, What is History, 31.

[151] Augustine himself was a judge by virtue of also having been a Bishop: this situation had been fashioned by Constantine that all Bishops of the Christian Church post-Nicaea were to act as civil appeal judges from whose chair cases on appeal from any Roman magistrate could be heard and given final judgment.

> evils he does not consider sins; for the wise judge does these things… because his ignorance compels him, and because human society claims him as a judge. …and had he any piety about him, he would cry to God, "From my necessities deliver Thou me."[152]
>
> But, say they, the wise man will wage just wars. As if he would not all the rather lament the necessity of just wars, if he remembers that he is a man; for if they were not just he would not wage them…. For it is the wrong-doing of the opposing party which compels the wise man to wage just wars….[153]

Augustine was a bishop-judge in the wake of the Constantinian reforms which included Christian Bishops taking on a judicial role which included being able to serve as judges in a final court of appeal for their own regions,[154] with only the Emperor above them for

---

[152] Augustine, *The City of God*, trans. Marcus Dods, George Wilson, and J.J. Smith, intro. Thomas Merton (New York: Modern Library – Random House, 1950), 19.6, 682-683.

[153] Ibid., 19.7, 683. The "But, say they…" in this passage refers most likely to Cicero and Plato, Augustine had a fingertip grasp of Cicero and would have almost as much command with Plato. We can see the philosophical and ideological foundations of the just-war concept, which would have been front and center in Augustine's mind when he wrote this, in Plato's *Republic* [Plato, Republic, *Plato: Complete Works*, trans. G.M.A. Grube and C.D.C Reeve, ed. John M. Cooper (Indianapolis/Cambridge: Hackett Publishing Company, 1997), 2.373.d-2.373.e, 1012] wherein Socrates explains to Glaucon how as the ideal city grows bigger there will be a need to take their neighbors' land and since the neighbors will want the same thing of them, war is the only way to either take land or defend one's land from being taken. The latter seems to lean in the direction of justified war, and Socrates says as much when he says that an large army will be required to defend the ideal city's substantial wealth (2.373.d-2.374.b, 1012-1013). Ironic here that the just war, defense of a city and its wealth, seems to be based on the unjust act of engaging in war to steal the neighbors land in the first place. Cicero takes glosses this more subtlety and specifically when he wrote:
...a war is never undertaken by the ideal state, except in defense of its honour or its safety…. …But private citizens often escape those punishments which even the most stupid can feel – poverty, exile, imprisonment and stripes – by taking refuge in a swift death. But in the case of a State, death itself is a punishment, though it seems to offer individuals an escape from punishment; for a State ought to be so firmly founded that it will live for ever. …Those wars are unjust which are undertaken without provocation. For only a war waged for revenge or defense can actually be just…. …No war is considered just unless it has been proclaimed and declared, or unless reparation has first been demanded…. …But our people by defending their allies have gained dominion over the whole world.
[Cicero, *De Re Publica De Legibus*, trans. Clinton Walker Keyes, (London: William Heinemann Ltd., 1977), III. xxiii, 210 – 213.] The dependent nature of Augustine's ideas is thus highlighted by the ideas of Plato/Socrates and Cicero.

[154] Church historian Sozomen writes, : "Constantine exempted the clergy everywhere from taxation, and permitted litigants to appeal to the decision of bishops if they preferred them to the state rulers. He enacted that their decree should be valid, and far superior to that of other judges as if pronounced by the emperor himself." Salaminius Hermias Sozomenus (Sozomen), *The Ecclesiastical History*, trans. Samuel Parker (1707), rev. Chester D. Hartranft, *A Select Library of Nicene and Post-Nicene Fathers of the Christian Church*, second ser., ed. Philip Schaff and Henry Wace, vol. 2, *Socrates, Sozomenus: Church Histories* (Peabody, Mass.: Hendrickson, 2004), 1.9, 246. See also a related account in, Eusebius of Caesarea, *Eusebius: Life of Constantine*, trans. Averil Cameron and Stuart G. Hall (Oxford: Clarendon Press, 1999) 4.27.2, 163.

last appeal: we learn here that Augustine's *nomos* was one in which the killing of innocents and just wars, involving the killing of innumerable people, were allowable "necessites" and not regarded as sin. By the time we reach Aquinas in the thirteenth century the killing of innocents and his concept of just war were at once both more widespread and more deeply entrenched in the meaningful order which that group had created for itself. The foregoing merely illustrates how powerful these meaningful orders become: they virtually sweep people along in their wake until a new order crushes the former and attempts to punish them retroactively for their crimes against humanity, which apparently are often not seen as crimes by the original perpetrators, for instance, in the case of the *Ancien Régime* in France and the subsequent French Revolution.

Yet as one might expect, there are a number of widely different orders or *nomos* instantiations which have run their course in various parts of the globe throughout history and very often within the same historical time period: one only has to think of his or her own lifetime to easily identify at least a few different such ones. Oftentimes these are competing orders that have gone to regrettable lengths to enforce their vision of the world. Mark Twain lays the case of multiple social orders competing with each other in his observation of some historical events occurring during the sixteenth century:

> For instance, when the Mississippi was first seen by [De Soto in 1542,].... Calvin, Benvenuto Cellini, and the Emperor Charles V. were at the top of their fame, and each was manufacturing history after his own peculiar fashion.... lax court morals and the absurd chivalry business were in full feather, and the joust and the tournament were the frequent pastime of titled fine gentlemen who could fight better than they could spell, while religion was the passion of their ladies, and the classifying of their offspring into children of full rank and children by brevet their pastime. In fact, all around, religion was in a particularly blooming condition: the Council of Trent was being called; the Spanish Inquisition was roasting, and racking, and burning, with a free hand; elsewhere on the Continent the nations were being persuaded to holy living by the sword and fire; in England, Henry VIII. had suppressed the monasteries, burned Fisher and another bishop or two, and was getting his English Reformation and his harem effectively started.[155]

Exactly correct: these were historically situated orders created by the likes of the above mentioned and all somewhat different in nature. We need remind ourselves that there has been and continues to be a multiplicity of social constructions of reality: the ones humanity is ultimately unable to bear are eventually, via other social constructions, put to rest.

155 Mark Twain, *The River and its History*, *Life on the Mississippi*, *The Writings of Mark Twain*, vol. IX, *Author's National Edition* (New York: Harper & Brothers Publishers, 1874; 1903), 19.

The problem in the relationship between human thought and other determinative factors within history which inform and delineate the borders of these orders is described by Berger as actually being a discovery made in historical scholarship within Germany of the nineteenth century, and is noted by Berger to be a "vertigo of relativity."[156] He writes:

> On the empirical level it led to the concern to investigate as painstakingly as possible the concrete relationships between thought and its historical situations. If this interpretation is correct, the sociology of knowledge takes up a problem originally posited by historical scholarship....[157]

While not a purely new question[158] it is interesting to note that from Berger's point of view in examining the roots of the sociology of knowledge, it was three nineteenth century developments in German thought which were the most important – the Marxian, the Nietzschean, and the historicist.[159] For our purposes, we recognize here his observation on the historicism of Wilhelm Dilthey which came immediately before his own sociology of knowledge, and its major theme was the ubiquitous sense of the relativity within all perspectives concerned with human events in history.[160] The historicist insistence was that no situation in history could be understood unless in its own terms.[161] This is similar to Bloch's observation that "...historical phenomenon can never be understood apart from its moment in time. This is true of every evolutionary stage, our own and all others. As the old Arab proverb has it: 'Men resemble their times more than they do their fathers.'"[162] Historicity also informs our knowledge within everyday life, in the sense that, for instance, we are born on a specific date, began school on another, etc., and these are located in a more comprehensive history of which our being in a location within that larger *nomos* shapes our situation.[163] Here we cross swords

---

156 Berger and Luckmann, *The Social Construction of Reality*, 4-5.

157 Ibid., 5.

158 Ibid. He points to antiquity for a beginning for the awareness of worldviews, and at least as far back as the enlightenment these investigations were a major theme.

159 Ibid.

160 Ibid., 6-7.

161 Ibid.

162 Bloch, *Historian's Craft*, 35.

163 Berger and Luckmann, *The Social Construction of Reality*, 27. Berger and Luckmann note a number of things pertinent to the social construction of reality which ought to be kept in mind: "The problem of legitimation inevitably arises when the objectivations of the (now historic) institutional order are to be transmitted to a new generation. At that point, as we have seen, the self-evident character of the institutions can no longer be maintained by means of the individual's own recollection and habitualization. The unity of history and biography is broken. In order to restore it, and thus to make intelligible both aspects of it, there must be "explanations" and justifications of the salient elements of the institutional tradition. Legitimation is this process of "explaining" and justifying." (86) This observation describes what was happening to early Christianity when the eye-witnesses to Jesus of Nazareth had virtually all passed on and we see a codification of belief system in both the early Christian writings (Gospels & Letters) and the bureaucracy which was raised to keep the tradition alive: the latter of which Constantine adopted to his

with the child of history and historicism, the sociology of knowledge, and it reminds us to be aware of the temporal structure regarding the historical person, event, or era before we reconstruct an explanatory suggestion about their nature and manifestations.

Also important are the symbolic universes, those sheltering canopies over individuals and institutions which set limits of what is relevant in social interaction.[164] With the symbolic canopy of the Christian religion of the fourth century permeating all levels of Roman life from the beggar to the emperor, for instance, we can see how such a 'universe' provided justification and a covering for the nascent Christian Roman Empire in all its manifestations, along with the almost immediate transformation within the bureaucracy of bishops from an organic and multivariate regional spiritual leadership to the role of judges and virtual prelates of their own realms of influence. Other major events later on in the story would figure in to this calcification of the Christian Church into a political entity as well, such as the influence of Augustine's (354-430) philosophy and vision for the Church on earth, the Frankish kings on the spread of an "orthodox" Christianity from the fifth to ninth centuries, the Great schism of 1054 in Christendom, and immediately following that the Investiture Contest beginning in 1057. In Constantine's Nicene episode, however, there was not only a Christian canopy being forced on to a Roman societal structure, there was also a Roman universe of ideals going the other way into the epicenter of the Christian Church. If such a confluence of symbolic universes was to be successful, it would link people "…with their predecessors and their successors in a meaningful totality, serving to transcend the finitude of individual existence and bestowing meaning upon the individual's death."[165] All people in this type of society think of themselves as being part of a meaningful universe which both preceded their own lives and will be there after they pass away and thus a physical community ascends to a spiritual plane and is made independent of the vicissitudes of

Empire – Berger and Luckmann describe this situation so pertinent to Constantine's adoptive act: "Historically, the problem of heresy has often been the first impetus for the systematic theoretical conceptualization of symbolic universes. The development of Christian theological thought as a result of a series of heretical challenges to the "official" tradition provides excellent historical illustrations for this process. … For instance, the precise Christological formulations of the early church councils were necessitated not by the tradition itself but by the heretical challenges to it. As these formulations were elaborated the tradition was maintained and expanded at the same time. Thus there emerged, among other innovations, a theoretical conception of the Trinity that was not only unnecessary but actually non-existent in the early Christian community." (99); "Societies have histories in the course of which specific identities emerge; these histories are, however, made by men with specific identities." (159); "…sociology must be carried on in a continuous convestaiont with tboth history and philosophy or lise its proper object of inquiry. This object is society as part of a human world, made by men, inhabited by men, and, in turn, making men, in an ongoing historical process. It is not the least fruit of a humanistic sociology that it reawakens our wonder at this astonishing phenomenon." (173).

164 Ibid., 94.

165 Ibid., 95.

life.[166] This is exactly the scenario of the later evolution of Constantine's new Romanized Christian Church who while on just such a cosmic plane and journey through the centuries could at the same time dispense with humane justice at will and replace it with their own dogmatic scheme which meant they "suffered" the suffering of others, but claimed it as necessary and legitimate under their larger cosmic nomos.

The creation of a symbolic universe is often given impetus by heretical ideas which challenge the "official" tradition,[167] or very much more likely, the most politically powerful group's assessment of what tradition actually is. Berger writes:

> For instance, the precise Christological formulations of the early church councils were necessitated not by the tradition itself but by the heretical challenges to it. As these formulations were elaborated, the tradition was maintained and expanded at the same time. Thus there emerged, among other innovations, a theoretical conception of the Trinity that was not only unnecessary but actually non-existent in the early Christian community. In other words, the symbolic universe is not only legitimated but also modified by the conceptual machineries constructed to ward off the challenge of heretical groups within a society.[168]

What modern historians now recognize as being almost a truism is that there was no such thing as a trinity doctrine taught either in the life of the early Church, or mentioned specifically in either Jewish Scriptures or the Christian writings in their possession. It was not the dominant belief of the Christian Church but merely one theological construction among others which seems to have emerged around the end of the second century.[169] As Berger says later of psychological theories that are concocted "before the fact," and their subsequent social establishment:[170] "Deliberate ideological manipulation by politically interested groups is one historical possibility."[171] The fact that the Alexandrian side of the debate at Nicaea won over at the time meant little to Constantine in comparison with his wish that the warring factions within Christianity made peace. Nicaea marked a new

[166] Ibid.

[167] Ibid., 99.

[168] Ibid.

[169] Origen of Alexandria (185-254) gives perhaps the strongest evidence in this regard, when he writes: Grant there may be some individuals among the multitudes of believers who are not in entire agreement with us, and who incautiously assert that the Saviour is the Most High God; however, we do not hold with them, but rather believe Him when He says, "The Father who sent Me is greater than I." We would not therefore make Him who we call Father inferior – as Celsus accuses us of doing – to the Son of God. Origen, *Origen Against Celsus*, in *Tertullian, Part Fourth; Minucius Felix; Commodian; Origen, Parts First and Second*, trans. Rev. Frederick Crombie, in *Ante-Nicene Fathers: The Writings of the Fathers Down to A.D. 325*, vol. 4, eds. Alexander Roberts and James Donaldson, rev. & arr. A. Cleveland Coxe (Peabody: Hendrickson Publishers, 1885), 8.14, 644.

[170] Ibid., 165.

[171] Ibid., 165.

beginning for the Christian Church: Constantine's adoption of it made it the Roman Christian Church.

In history, in actual history, that entity which is physically lost to historians in the same way the ideal Forms were physically unavailable to Socrates and Plato, change happens by definition;[172] but every once in a while a massive change, such as the marriage of Church and State under Constantine, takes place. The scholar most identified as having studied and named this large scale change phenomenon is science historian Thomas S. Kuhn (1922-1996): he was the creator of the much employed notion of "paradigm shift". What is a paradigm, what does he mean by 'shift,' and then what does their confluence suggest? In his monograph *The Structure of Scientific Revolutions* he describes his use of paradigm throughout the book as consisting of two senses:

> On the one hand it stands for the entire constellation of beliefs, values, techniques, and so on shared by the members of a given community. On the other, it denotes one sort of element in that constellation, the concrete puzzle-solutions which, employed as models or examples, can replace explicit rules as a basis for the solution of the remaining puzzles of normal science.[173]

By "normal science" Kuhn means simply a paradigm in operation.[174] But when a scientific community is forced to replace explicit rules and assumptions, when the profession can no longer ignore the anomalies that have thwarted the ruling paradigm, an extraordinary shift of commitments occurs which, according to Kuhn, results in a scientific revolution.[175] "They are the tradition-shattering complements to the tradition-bound activity of normal science."[176] The scientific turning points attributed to Copernicus and Einstein, for instance, are paradigmatic cases of scientific revolution because they necessitated a rejection of an established theory for a new and better one that was, notwithstanding its familiarity to revolutionary protagonists, incompatible with the former; these breakthroughs also resulted in a fundamental shift in the problems and problem solutions which would henceforth count as admissible; and finally, these historical events transformed the imagination of scholars which consequently transformed the very world in which their work was being done.[177] Stanislav Andreski describes the nature of some of these monumental shifts:

> The proliferation of apparatus of physical research which has taken place during the last quarter of a century has not led, I am told by my physicist friends, to any

172 See discussion above on change and continuity pursuant to observations by Gustavson.
173 Thomas S. Kuhn, *The Structure of Scientific Revolutions*, 2nd ed., enlarged (Chicago: University of Chicago Press, 1962; 1975), 175.
174 Ibid., 11. For Kuhn's complete discussion of normal science see sections II, III, and IV: 10-42.
175 Ibid., 6.
176 Ibid.
177 Ibid.

> fundamental discoveries which could be compared in originality to the contributions which Rutherford, Planck, Bohr or Heisenberg made with much smaller resources – not to speak of Einstein, who produced his relativity theory in his spare time and without access to a laboratory, while working for the Swiss patent office, after having been turned down as a candidate for a higher degree. There is nothing inexplicable in this, because organization involves subordination and dependence not only on the seniors but on the peers and even juniors as well, while the entire history of science abundantly demonstrates that really original ideas have nearly always met with obstinate resistance from the majority of the specialists.[178]

Andreski portrays Kuhn's "tradition-bound" specialists standing in the way of certainly anomalous but, more importantly, original ideas which ultimately replace the basic assumptions and rules of the field upon which the genius, for instance, of Einstein was momentarily thwarted in the *denial of access to graduate studies.* Achievements on this scale from the likes of Copernicus and Einstein are then of great importance to the historian who is trying to reconstruct the story of what actually happened 'ever after' in the permanent alteration of the landscape by the new paradigm.[179]

---

[178] Andreski, *Social Sciences as Sorcery*, 187. He writes elsewhere: "The history of all the sciences amply demonstrates that the more original the idea, the greater the resistance it has met. We all know about Copernicus' fear of the stake, the tribulations of Galileo, the vituperations against Darwin, the horror which greeted Harvey's deviation from Galen's medical bible, and the attempts to oust Pasteur from the medical profession. Many other examples could be added: Einstein's having been turned down as a candidate for graduate studies, or the failure of Newton's early attempts to secure a fellowship in Cambridge, of Lobatchevsky being taken for a lunatic after he announced his discovery of non-Euclidean geometry. There are even more extreme cases: of the great mathematician, Abel, starving throughout almost his entire life and dying prematurely in consequence; of Gallous failing (twice, if I remember rightly) an entrance examination to a university in mathematics, a subject in which he had already laid the foundations for an entirely new branch now known as the theory of groups." (195). Bloch writes something similar when he notes, "Nor would it be wise to rely entirely upon academic bodies for these instruments [copies of source documents, second hand sources, etc.], for their methods of recruiting, favoring seniority and orthodox scholarship, do not particularly incline them to a spirit of enterprise." (70). While it is granted that Bloch wrote this in the early 1940s and that in many universities tremendous advances in fairness and egalitarianism and access to knowledge have been made, we still must remember that human actors continue to make the decisions which were so roundly and rightly criticized by the likes of Block and Andreski. To think we in our own day are less likely to fall prey to human weaknesses because of the advances made in the rule of law, human rights, etc., is a foreboding generalization indeed.

[179] Kuhn, *Scientific Revolutions*: Other interesting observations Kuhn makes to further delineate what his paradigm shift was after include, while not be limited to, the following: "…the perception of anomaly – of a phenomenon, that is, for which his paradigm had not readied the investigator – played an essential role in preparing the way for perception of novelty. But, again in both cases, the perception that something had gone wrong was only the prelude to discovery." (57); "Both during pre-paradigm periods and during the crises that lead to large-scale changes of paradigm, scientists usually develop many speculative and unarticulated theories that can themselves point the way to discovery. …. Only as experiment and tentative

Each field of study, according to Kuhn, has at one time crossed over from its pre-history to its history proper and while many of these transitions are not as sudden as the idea of paradigm shift may imply, neither were they gradual and coextensive with the fields in which they occurred.[180] The entity/discovery does not develop gradually as with an island forming from bubbling lava over thousands of years, as historical events do for some for historians who claim everything humankind has experienced in terms of advances in science, medicine, and technology is mere accretion – and we can see the adherence to this idea even in rudimentary form in an aspect of the historical method itself which claims every event is both connected with the past and yet a departure from it. Kuhn's idea is a significant challenge to those scholars who interpret historical events, discoveries, and revolutions as nothing more than the result of an accretion of past events instead of radical departures with little or nothing to do with past practice or assumptions. For instance, Marc Bloch wrote that it is a fallacy to "… [represent] the course of human evolution as a series of short violent jerks, no one of which exceeds the space of a few lifetimes. Observation proves, on the contrary, that the mighty convulsions of that vast, continuing development are perfectly capable of extending from the beginning of time to the present."[181] Yet Bloch does insist that "it is change which the historian is seeking to grasp,"[182] but Kuhn is only asking we separate those few times where the changes are so radical as to belong to another category. Kuhn does not say all changes should be accorded paradigm revolution status, nothing of the sort: but in his particular field of science he noticed four or five over three thousand years which were such radical breaks with past assumptions as to be accorded the strong language of "shift." It is as if a massive earthquake fifty-thousand years ago slammed one small

---

theory are together articulated to a match does the discovery emerge and the theory become a paradigm." (61); [Three important characteristics which result in discoveries from which new phenomena emerge are] "…the previous awareness of anomaly, the gradual and simultaneous emergence of both observational and conceptual recognition, and the consequent change of paradigm categories and procedures often accompanied by resistance." (62); "Because it demands large-scale paradigm destruction and major shifts in the problems and techniques of normal science, the emergence of new theories is generally preceded by a period of pronounced professional insecurity. As one might expect, that insecurity is generated by the persistent failure of the puzzles of normal science to come out as they should. Failure of existing rules is the prelude to a search for new ones." (67-68); "…crises are a necessary precondition for the emergence of novel theories…. Though they [scholars] may begin to lost faith and then to consider alternatives, they do not renounce the paradigm that has led them into crisis." (77); [This following quote appears to the author to be Kuhn's first use of the phrase] "…the switch of gestalt, particularly because it is today so familiar, is a useful elementary prototype for what occurs in full-scale paradigm shift." (85);

[180] Ibid., 21. He writes in another place, "…discovery involves an extended, though not necessarily long, process of conceptual assimilation. Can we say it involves a change in paradigm? …yes" [specifically in regards to the discovery of oxygen, but generally to all significant paradigm shifts of this nature]: 56.

[181] Bloch, *Historian's Craft*, 41. Bloch gives a concrete example in noting "…who would dare to say that the understanding of the Protestant or the Catholic Reformation several centuries removed, is not far more important for a proper grasp of the world today than a great many other movements of thought or feeling, which are certainly more recent, yet more ephemeral?" (41).

[182] Ibid., 46.

continent from into the coast of a large one and henceforth became part of the latter: we might imagine a group of *Homo sapiens sapiens* from the island that would now discover wholly new creatures and environments which their previous isolation made the discovery of impossible.

While Kuhn was not sure about how his paradigm shift notion would fare in other disciplines,[183] other scholars have expropriated his ideas by fiat due to its attractive generalizability pursuant to other fundamental shifts. Beyond this, as well, I think not having to use the word "revolution" was a breath of fresh air to scholars wishing to describe world changing events without reference to an idea so inextricably tied to the notion of war. Applied to my own research on Constantine's adoption of the Christian Church and bureaucracy, the idea of paradigm shift, or paradigm revolution as Kuhn himself referred to it, fits my Roman Emperor's changes rather convincingly. Kuhn himself writes:

> Political revolutions aim to change political institutions in ways that those institutions themselves prohibit. Their success therefore necessitates the partial relinquishment of one set of institutions in favor of another, and in the interim, society is not fully governed by institutions at all. Initially it is crisis alone that attenuates the role of political institutions as we have already seen it attenuate the role of paradigms. In increasing numbers individuals become increasingly estranged from political life and behave more and more eccentrically within it. Then, as the crisis deepens, many of these individuals commit themselves to some concrete proposal for the reconstruction of society in a new institutional framework. At that point the society is divided into competing camps or parties, one seeking to defend the old institutional constellation, the others seeking to institute some new one. And, once that polarization has occurred, *political recourse fails*. Because they differ about the institutional matrix within which political change is to be achieved and evaluated, because they acknowledge no supra-institutional framework for the adjudication of revolutionary difference, the parties to a revolutionary conflict must finally resort to the techniques of mass persuasion, often including force.[184]

---

[183] Kuhn, *Scientific Revolutions*, 208. Kuhn writes, "A number of those who have taken pleasure from it have done so less because it illuminates science than because they read its main theses as applicable to many other fields as well. I see what they mean and would not like to discourage their attempts to extend the position, but their reaction has nevertheless puzzled me. To the extent that the book portrays scientific development as a succession of tradition bound periods punctuated by non-cumulative breaks, its theses are undoubtedly of wide applicability. But they should be, for they are borrowed from other fields. Historians of literature, of music, of the arts, of political development, and of many other human activities have long described their subjects in the same way. Periodization in terms of revolutionary breaks in style, taste, and institutional structure have been among their standard tools."

[184] Kuhn, *Scientific Revolutions*, 93.

In reference to Constantine's revolution of the Roman world, I could not have put it better myself. Another scholar who is also convinced of the confluence between Kuhn's characterization of "shift" and Constantine's reorganization of the relationship between Church and State is noted historian John Howard Yoder. In fact, one of Yoder's most important contributions to historical studies is what he named the "Constantinian Shift,"[185] referring to this historical period where the Roman and Christian worlds merge under the Emperor's orders.

John Howard Yoder's seminal identification of a "Constantinian shift" refers specifically to the way the Church both viewed itself and the world, and its role in the world. Constantine is not the sole architect, according to Yoder, but he is the symbol for the shift itself continuing to permeate through the centuries after his reign right up until the present day. Yoder's main observations on the "shift" are the following: First, before Constantine one saw Christian communities, a variety of them at that, which took it on faith that God was governing history, while after Constantine you had to have faith that there was a true Christian community amongst the masses of nominal "Christians" and ecclesiastic types. Second, Christendom paints a thin veneer of religiosity and sanctity on the new sovereignty order, the new construction, the new dominance, and the language, but it leaves untouched the very culture it aimed to convert. Late antiquity Europe and Asia adopt the name of Christian but know nothing of Jesus and the communal, minority, visible life of the early church. All is wiped clean by the wrath of what became known as "orthodoxy." Third, the future ramifications turned out to be even worse, if that were possible, in the reality of Crusade. These apocalyptic events made the outsider an infidel, the epitome of anti-faith. To destroy another person who also feared God became virtuously exemplary. The Christian world of the crusades had a "divinely" imparted duty to destroy or to rule over their world.[186] In describing his suggestion of shift Yoder writes "...the fact that with Constantine the civil sovereign becomes God's privileged agent is thus not merely a shift in accent but a change of direction."[187]

Yoder's analysis goes to heart of the shift in practice and doctrine within the Christian Church as it made its radical move away from spiritual disciplines towards temporal political power, and he is correct in identifying Constantine as the progenitor around which so many of the changes orbited. Anthropologically, and keeping in mind both Kuhn and Yoder's observations relating to Constantine's colossal shift in governance, religion, and law within his Empire beginning in earnest at Nicaea, there is another scholar who made a significant contribution to the discussion of how and why these

---

185 John Howard Yoder, *The Constantinian Sources of Western Social Ethics. The Priestly Kingdom: Social Ethics as Gospel* (Notre Dame, Indianna: University of Notre Dame Press, 1984).
186 Ibid.
187 Ibid., 139.

shifts take place, Anthony F.C. Wallace. Wallace points to what he suggests can be thought of as "Revitalization Movements."[188] He writes:

> A revitalization movement is defined as a deliberate, organized, conscious effort by members of a society to construct a more satisfying culture. Revitalization is thus, from a cultural standpoint, a special kind of culture change phenomenon: the persons involved in the process of revitalization must perceive their culture, or some major areas of it, as a system (whether accurately or not); they must feel that this cultural system is unsatisfactory; and they must innovate not merely discrete items, but a new cultural system, specifying new relationships as well as, in some cases, new traits. The classic processes of culture change (evolution, drift, diffusion, historical change, acculturation) all produce changes in cultures as systems; however, they do not depend on deliberate intent by members of a society, but rather on a gradual chain-reaction effect.... In revitalization movements, however [these effects] are shifted into a new Gestalt abruptly and simultaneously in intent; and frequently within a few years the new plan is put into effect by the participants in the movement.[189]

You can see clearly here the parallel between Kuhn's and Wallace's ideas and language. Notice Wallace's "...shifted into a new Gestalt abruptly..." and there you have Kuhn, only this time from an anthropological standpoint. Wallace's theory also aligns with Kuhn's in rejecting the idea that everything in the historical narrative is mere accretion, yet Wallace claims that it would be very few generations indeed that were not witness *to* or involved *in* some form of revitalization process.[190] For Wallace, his main focus was how the process of revitalization movements appears in cultures throughout history via the instrumentality of the births of new religions or the splitting of old ones. In this way Wallace's theory relates that much closer to my own research on the marriage of Constantine's Empire and its peoples to the Christian Church.

Wallace is careful to point out that the existing literature of his time had already dealt with smaller movements that he identifies as subclasses in contrast to what he describes as the large scale phenomena, revitalization movements.[191] If we observe what he

[188] Anthony F.C. Wallace, "Revitalization Movements," *American Anthropologist* 58 (1956): 264-281.
[189] Ibid., 265.
[190] Ibid., 267. In this sense Wallace's theory can be differentiated from Kuhn's because the latter notes that it was only a rare occurrence in his own field of history of science.
[191] Wallace notes research that had been done previous to or contemporaneously with his own that dealt with smaller "subclass" phenomena. He points to the following: Natavistic Movements - Linton, Ralph, "Natavistic movements," *American Anthropologist* 45 (1943): 230-240; Revivalistic movements - James Mooney, *The Ghost Dance Religion. Bureau of American Ethnology Annual Report* (Washington: 1892-93); Cargo cults – F.E. Williams, *The Vailala Madness and the Destruction of Native Ceremonies in the Gulf Division* (Port Moresby, Territory of Papua: Anthropology No. 4): 192 & F.E. Williams, *The Vailala Madness in Retrospect.* In *Essays Presented to C.G. Seligman* (London: 1934); Millenarian and Messianic movements - Wilson D.

referred to as the "processual structure" we see parallel's not only with Kuhn's paradigm shift but also with my own research on Constantine and the ruling apparatus of the fourth century Christian Church. Wallace suggests five stages for his revitalization movement. First is a "Steady State," wherein most citizens of a society take advantage of culturally recognized techniques for satisfying social needs that work well enough that chronic stress varies within tolerable limits.[192] This is followed in turn by a period of "Increased Individual Stress" in which individuals experience critical levels of stress because of the deficiencies of existing stress reduction instrumentalities.[193] A point is then reached where another way has to be considered, and the very consideration of it causes more stress because members of the society may wonder whether it will be even worse than the first. Third comes a period of "Cultural Distortion," marked by people of tradition being willing to abide high levels of chronic stress rather than trying to solve the problems within the mazeway[194] – the mazeway being an individual's mental image of the society and culture as well as his or her own body and its behavioural regularities which cause them to act in ways that reduce stress at all levels of the societal system.[195] People not endeared with tradition try mazeway changes to reduce the stress with varying degrees of concern for the wholeness or Gestalt of the system. The culture is internally distorted in this stage and stress continues to rise leading finally to a recognition that the existing stress reduction mechanisms are failing, and "…as the internal incongruities of the mazeway are perceived, symptoms of anxiety over the loss of a meaningful way of life also become evident: disillusionment with the mazeway, and apathy toward problems of adaptation, set in."[196] The fourth stage is one of "Revitalization," and now in spite of the portent of society's end seemingly looming, a revitalization movement, many being religious in character, comes to forestall disaster. The fifth state is simply the new steady state, but it is the fourth stage which is most crucial according to Wallace.

These religious revitalization movements, and focusing on his fourth stage of 'revitalization,' must perform six major tasks,[197] and because they parallel's Constantine's restructuring of the Roman world, we will observe and note the generally relevant events

---

Wallis, *Messiahs - Christian and Pagan* (Boston: 1918) & Wilson D. Wallis, *Messiahs, Their Role in Civilization* (Washington: 1943).

192 Wallace, *Revitalization Movements*, 268.

193 Ibid., 269.

194 Ibid.

195 Ibid., 266. On "Mazeway," Wallace earlier cites some of his earlier work as well as that of A.I. Hallowell. A.I. Hallowell, "The Self and Its Behavioral Environment," *Culture and Experience* (Philadelphia, 1955); Anthony F.C. Wallace, "The Disruption of the Individual's Identification with his Culture in Disasters and other Extreme Situations," Paper read at National Research Council, Committee on Disaster Studies, *Conference on Theories of Human Behavior in Extreme Situations* (Vassar College, 1955); Wallace, *The Mazeway*, *Explorations* No. 6, 1956).

196 Wallace, *Revitalization Movements*, 270.

197 Ibid., see discussion at 270-275.

in turn. The first task is mazeway reformulation, which involves a restructuring of elements and dependent systems already either in use or accepted and which are known to a person who becomes the prophet/leader. These restructurings are usually preceded by one or a number of hallucinatory visions by a single person. With Constantine, we have an exemplar of this category, who received the penultimate experience of having a vision – as well as subsequent dreams – of Christ as he stared into the sun's glare, and receiving the advice that he would triumph with the banner of the cross – something like "in this sign you will conquer."[198] The second task is for the prophet-leader to communicate his revelations. Following his Council at Nicaea – and the reader must understand that this was a private affair between Constantine and Christian Bishops, there were no galleries for the lay people, and the Roman Senate had no representatives there that we know of, but we do know that many of Constantine's officers and soldiers from his army were there, as one can imagine – Constantine sent letters throughout his Empire, one for the Christians and one for those outside Christianity which both explained his new conviction about the efficacy of the Christian God and his Son Christ in both giving him victory in war over societal tyrants and also being able to produce a more stable and moral Roman society. Thirdly in Wallace's rubric of revitalization movements is the task of organization, an assignment carried out by a small subset of the faithful, some of whom just happen to be already influential people in society. Constantine's Christian bishops, who had gravitated to him at the beginning of his initial adoption of the religion, and during his victorious war campaigns in the Western Empire, are well known to historians – Ossius of Cordoba, Eusebius of Caesarea, and Eusebius of Nicomedia being the most well-known. Bishops following the Nicene episode were given the power of regional appeal judges as well, further strengthening Constantine's personal control of society due to the allegiance owed Constantine by the Bishops pursuant to his deliverance of the Christian religion from persecution to political power. The fourth task, according to Wallace, is adaption which is often necessitated by resistance of some sort. Wallace writes "the movement may therefore have to use various strategies of adaptation: doctrinal modification; political and diplomatic maneuver; and force.

Anyone familiar with the Constantinian reformation of Roman society will know that he practiced all three: changing the doctrine was accomplished, as Berger pointed out above, by allowing a small faction to change the Christian doctrine to a triune God rather than Father and Son as Constantine had first understood it; political maneuver can be seen in his making bishops judges and changing the appeal system of Roman law so

[198] Of course, of the Roman Empire of this period, those that were not Christians were not being coerced into Constantine's new religion, but a major section of his population was Christian, and whole legions in the Roman army were known to be Christian. This was only the beginning of the emperor's adoption of Christianity, and it would take some time before the rest of the non-Christian population caught up to the new status quo, perhaps thirty years or so, nearer the time of Theodosius II (401-450).

as to keep tighter control on abuses at the local level; the force factor can be lost on no one who knows of his murder of his own son, wife, and his *Edict Against the Heretics* which demanded a number of groups cease and desist and turn over their properties to the new Christian order. The fifth stage of "cultural transformation" is one wherein the large shift has been accepted by the controlling elements of a society and wherein successful projects of social, political, or economic reform are instituted. This found expression in the restoration of property to the Christian Church and the massive benefactions and expense funds then made available to the Christian Church by Constantine. The sixth and final stage is a routinization involving a pan-societal acceptance of the religion's establishment as the religion attempts to confine itself to doctrine and ritual. This was certainly the case at the beginning of the Church State relationship in terms of the Bishops ostensibly being confined to religious issues, yet due to Constantine's benefactions of civil power on the Bishops, the latter only grew more politically powerful as the Roman Empire of the West began to fall in earnest less than one-hundred years later.

As with Constantine's revitalization movement, himself as the star prophet-leader along with attendant vision and dreams, most such movements are more or less grounded in a particular religious matrix of one kind or another, with perhaps the notable exception of Russian communist movements and others in this strain. Yet as Wallace points out, "…the quality of doctrine and of leader-follower relationships is so similar, at least on superficial inspection, to religious doctrine and human-supernatural relations, that one wonders whether it is not a distinction without a difference."[199] Wallace wonders whether, in a world in which human affairs are decided with less and less reference to supernatural powers, religious revitalization movements can be dispensed with before reaching some kind of peace/utopia without the attendant stresses and strains[200] so clearly seen in all of history so far. He thinks that while it is the case that religious movements do involve crude and powerful emotions and fantasies of relationships with supernatural beings which occasionally lead to unfortunate consequences in human relationships, these same fantasies and emotions may have worse consequences for peace and human rights when directed toward people – political or ideological leaders – seen in similar lights.[201] He is right that religious movements do lead to unfortunate consequences in human relationships: one only has to think of Constantine's legacy to the Church in their Crusades, Witch hunts, Inquisitions, and torture and killing of Christians outside of their own *nomos*. The major religions have now mostly been reined

[199] Ibid., 277.

[200] Ibid.

[201] Ibid., 277-278. Wallace writes: "The answer would seem to be as fewer and fewer [people] make use of the religious displacement process, there will have to be a corresponding reduction of the incidence and severity of transference neuroses, or human relationships will be increasingly contaminated by character disorders, neurotic acting out, and paranoid deification of political leaders and ideologies." [One

in by the enlightenment informed humanist dictates of the state[202] and yet there are still sizeable groups in various parts of the world that are committed to their own version of a religion and they have proven willing to "kill for peace." Thankfully, for most religions, these barbarities have been swept away by the enlightenment and revolutionary periods in Western Europe, the former being an ideology of sorts which put the human being and their rights and safety before any fantastical religious considerations.

The analogous question we must ask along with Wallace's own, is whether current attachments to new ideologies and various institutions will lead to a safer world with less attendant strain and stress for the individual? Are character disorders, neurotic acting out, and deification of political leaders and ideologies on the rise? And if a reined-in religious group can stick to offering the comforting teachings of their prophet and a sense of purpose within a community of meaning and yet also swear off the use of force, perhaps Wallace is right to wonder whether we may after all be better off allowing religion to play its part in alleviating social stresses[203] for the individual rather than pretending that multivariate ideologies and/or the deification of political leaders will result in the elusive peace the world seeks. But if, as he sets out as two possible preconditions, there is "high stress for individual members of the society, and disillusionment with a distorted cultural Gestalt…"[204] then a revitalization movement will be necessary, in keeping with the processual structure and rubric of stages discussed above.

The historian then ought to recognize in his or her own investigations into events far removed from their own day that the aspects and stages of change suggested by the likes of Kuhn and Wallace are very helpful in creating a generalized framework which can then be applied for comparison and reflection and perhaps ultimately lead to tentative conclusions about how well or not those generalizable theories account for the historical data available. These conclusions can then be recast as suggestions, combined with other researches, as to "what happened" in any particular historical event at issue.

Legal actors, as well, faced with the often difficult task of reconstructing past events and aiming to bring justice based on law in a particular situation can benefit from many of the foregoing hermeneutical tools in that these members within the justice system are charged with the task of understanding the context of an event involving persons to the best of their ability. It is very likely that legal actors would be better served by recognizing the salient aspects of the method described above in helping them

---

202 Of course this is a great irony since most of the dictates/laws of the state, and certainly the actions of beneficent non-profit organizations, pertaining to human rights stem mostly, at least in the Western experience, from the Jewish and Christian Scriptures.
203 Ibid., This is implied by Wallace at 277-278.
204 Ibid., 279.

understand the complexities implicit in the contexts of the lives and actions of those for whom they are called upon to defend, prosecute, and deliver judgements upon.

Final Thoughts

Marc Bloch poignantly noted,

> Are we so sure of ourselves and of our age as to divide the company of our forefathers in the just and the damned? How absurd it is, by elevating the entirely relative criteria of one individual, one party, or one generation to the absolute, to inflict standards upon the way in which Sulla governed Rome, or Richelieu the States of the Most Christian King! …. Robespierrists! Anti-Robespierrists! For pity's sake, simply tell us what Robespierre was.[205]

So while we may not judge as historians, we can employ history in helping us make better judgements. So too, the legal actor employs history in helping them make better judgments, and since they *are* required to ultimately come up with a judgment, their attention to the method by which they understand the various contexts put before them is of paramount importance. Carr suggests that "[t]he past is intelligible to us only in the light of the present; and we can fully understand the present only in the light of the past. To enable man to understand the society of the past, and to increase his mastery over the society of the present, is the dual function of history."[206] As we have observed, there are subtle differences of opinion amongst historians as to what we can expect from history, but there is general agreement on how it should best be constructed.

I have suggested that a synthesis of some of the most important contributions to historical method is something well within the reach of a historian, and I have cast it roughly as follows: the historical method I aim for requires an imaginative re-construction of an historical event and its concomitant personages which is based on extant data, but which also must engage in a participatory re-thinking pursuant to the motivations of the characters involved such that the end result can be read as an intelligible whole. The historian has no access to actual history, with the exception of their own of which they form a part. But if that is the case, they are actually only part of history as a result of their participation in the present. Once a moment passes, it departs into the metaphysical, it cannot be revisited or recaptured with any hope of total accuracy. But it is the metaphysical existence of actual history, that ideal form, which historians are most concerned to reflect in their own suggestions: they hope they are striking as close to that ideal form as possible.

205 Bloch, *Historian's Craft*, 140.

206 Carr, *What is History?*, 55; see also page 68.

Historians use real non-metaphysical evidence from that illusive actual history to reconstruct the lives of people who are, for the most part, unless you are studying the history of someone still living, no longer able to inform us about what actually happened. Yet this kind of documentary and physical evidence often provides historians with enough congruent information that we can be relatively certain about the main brush strokes of what was going on in, for instance, Rome during the early fourth century. The less information we have about a place or person, the less which can be suggested, but the opposite case produces reconstructions by historians which are sufficiently close enough to what the general consensus of the extant evidence demands that they must be accepted as reasonable suggestions about what most likely happened at a given moment in history. So while actual history is illusive, the lower orders of the ideal history based on corroborated evidence often produces from the pen of a historian a very satisfactory and intelligibly whole account of what most likely took place. Historians and readers of history must be satisfied with this middle ground of 'reasonably sure' with regard to events that have passed. As already pointed out, the writing of history is not like a criminal trial wherein the judge demands evidence which she or her jury must be convinced of beyond a reasonable doubt. History is much more like a civil trial where the judge or jury is satisfied that the evidence bears out a given claim on a 'balance of probabilities,' a much lower standard of proof than 'beyond a reasonable doubt.'

History is not then out of reach completely. But like the word 'history' itself demands, the process of writing history will always be to some degree about constructing a story. In the foregoing discussion I have emphasized my suggestion that some of these stories, these responsible reconstructions of past events based on a sound historical method, are as close as we are ever going to get to what actually happened: and, in the absence of new evidence which might throw their conclusions into doubt, for this reason they ought reasonably to be taken seriously.

Made in the USA
Monee, IL
08 November 2026

68032034R00069

Praise for *Unleash Your Crazy To Win*

"Vicki is an amazing human being with an unprecedented spirit. In her book *Unleash Your Crazy To Win* Vicki demonstrates the power of positive thinking and how she beat the odds by overcoming personal and professional adversity. It is a remarkable read. I read it cover to cover and was intrigued by its uniqueness. With this book Vicki inspires, gives hope and demonstrates the power of the human spirit. Vicki neatly weaves together two remarkable stories of personal and professional adversity that demonstrate the power of intention. The result is awesome."

—Kevin McFadden
President, McFadden Benefits & Pension

"I thoroughly enjoyed this book and read it with a lot of curiosity. Vicki has a way of taking her real-life experiences and sharing them to help others. There is some concrete stuff here that really applies to our own lives."

—Michelle Sawatzky-Koop,
Radio Host - Golden West Radio,
1996 Olympian, Mother of twins

"Infertility is a topic not often written about because of the stigma of failure that goes with it. Vicki shares very personal stories about her journey, about making tough decisions, the pain and joy along the way, and overcoming odds in both her personal and business life. She has her OMG moments, educates and inspires us to sometimes ignore logic and instead listen to our hearts."

—Ryan Anderson, Life Coach

"*Unleash Your Crazy To Win* boldly addresses a taboo subject that cuts across culture, race and religion. It is a true story of one woman's battle to overcome infertility resulting in the birth of not one, but two healthy and beautiful children; fearless, riveting and unapologetic. I couldn't put it down until I turned the last page, and even then it wouldn't let me go. If you are looking for a "How to *Overcome*" instructional when faced with the impossible, then this is the book to read — Vicki's story *resonated.*"

—Banjo Aromolaran-Eaton, Business Owner

"Absolutely brilliant book. Impossible things really can become possible. You've just got to believe and then bring out the *Crazy* in you until it happens."

—Chino Okeem, Director, Mary Kay

"If you are someone looking for excuses to stick with the status quo... to accept a no when there is still the possibility... then this book is not for you! *Unleash Your Crazy To Win* is real – Vicki not only tells us how she overcame a personal challenge that affects so many couples, she also shares all the hurt and pain she went through. She shares her vulnerability in a way many would not be able to. Although this book refers specifically to infertility, the feelings and frustrations could be associated with any personal health issue and as such, the book is universal. I think Vicki's message comes through loud and clear every page of the book – never give up!"

—Fumi Popoola, Tax Accountant